A Pastoral Theology of Childlessness

A Pastoral Theology of Childlessness

Emma Nash

scm press

© Emma Nash 2021

Published in 2021 by SCM Press
Editorial office
3rd Floor, Invicta House,
108–114 Golden Lane,
London EC1Y 0TG, UK
www.scmpress.co.uk

SCM Press is an imprint of Hymns Ancient & Modern Ltd
(a registered charity)

Hymns Ancient & Modern® is a registered trademark of
Hymns Ancient & Modern Ltd
13A Hellesdon Park Road, Norwich,
Norfolk NR6 5DR, UK

Scripture quotations are from New Revised Standard Version
Bible: Anglicized Edition, copyright © 1989, 1995 National
Council of the Churches of Christ in the United States of America.
Used by permission. All rights reserved worldwide.

British Library Cataloguing in Publication data

A catalogue record for this book is available
from the British Library

978-0-334-06051-2

Typeset by Regent Typesetting
Printed and bound by
CPI Group (UK) Ltd

For Shona, Melanie and Jacky.
You shared my sadness and, in sharing it,
you made it easier to bear.

And for Derek, best friend and co-traveller
on the lonely journey

Contents

Introduction

Jacob was left alone; and a man wrestled with him until daybreak. When the man saw that he did not prevail against Jacob, he struck him on the hip socket; and Jacob's hip was put out of joint as he wrestled with him. Then he said, 'Let me go, for the day is breaking.' But Jacob said, 'I will not let you go, unless you bless me.' (Gen. 32.24–26)

As a person of faith struggling with childlessness, I have had a deep need to understand my experience before God. This book is part of the outcome of my own wrestling over the past six years. I have felt abandoned, unloved, overlooked, cursed, embittered and lonely. I have been in great need of blessing.[1] Many of my underlying beliefs about God, life and what it means to have faith have been profoundly undermined. As I have wrestled with God, I have come to understand that God is not my enemy. In times of trouble, some people find themselves doubting God's very existence: I do not judge them. Personally, I never doubted that God was there, but I was very, very angry. I felt that God had let me down. I do not feel that any more, but it has taken me a while to get to this point.

This book is not a memoir, although I will frequently refer to elements of my own story. It was my experience of childlessness that demanded theological reflection of which the book is a product. One of the places where I sought healing, once it became clear that my infertility was likely to be permanent, was the library. I struggled to find books that would help me, however. I found devotional works that encouraged me to trust God but which, for me, failed to engage with the apparent indifference and inaction of God and with the ugly depths of rage, desperation and hopelessness to which my childlessness sent me. I found excellent books that did engage with this pain and ugliness and which greatly helped me, but not being written from a faith perspective they did not help me discern the presence of God in my experience. For me, the best theological work on childlessness has been written by Kevin Ellis, most notably in his Grove Booklet, *Christianity and Childlessness* (Ellis 2006). Inspired by Ellis's work, I have set about the task of a longer and more developed treatment of the subject.

Another writer whose work has greatly influenced this book is the American trauma theologian, Serene Jones. She writes of 'the balmlike work of theology and of religion' to uncover wounds and to bring healing (Jones 2009, p. 1). In a beautiful chapter exploring reproductive loss, Jones explains: 'We wanted images, a drama, a story, a vivid language that could draw together our strange experience … and the faith and feminism, which have so profoundly formed us' (Jones 2009, p. 128). This is what I have attempted to do in this book: to uncover the wounds of infertility and childlessness; to apply images and stories from Scripture to this experience; to seek, and perhaps to find healing in the process.

This pastoral theology of childlessness has resolved itself into five main areas of reflection. In Chapter 1 I examine the *isolation* experienced by people struggling with childlessness, an isolation that can be deepened rather than eased by reading the Scriptures. In Chapter 2 I attempt a *theology of pain*, rooted in reflection on the three-day event of the cross and resurrection, including the pause between them, the often-neglected Holy Saturday. In Chapter 3 I consider the theme of *power*, exploring the profound powerlessness experienced by people who cannot conceive a child, or whose pregnancies end in early loss. I consider several unanswered prayers found in the Bible, and ask what it might mean to trust God when we feel we cannot be sure God wants to help us, or even is able to. In Chapter 4 I reflect on the themes of *barrenness and fruitfulness*, asking how we might live up to our calling as co-creators with God when we cannot create new life, no matter how hard we try. In Chapter 5 I consider *medical ethics*, outlining some of the ethical dilemmas involved in fertility treatment and asking how we might begin to navigate them. Chapters 1–5 begin with the lived experience, move on to look for consolation in the Bible and Christian theology, and end by asking what liberative practice might look like in the light of this reflection. Finally, in Chapter 6, I offer some suggestions for good practice in churches.

This book has been written so that followers of Jesus might respond to the crisis of involuntary childlessness in ways that are life-giving and that point to the presence of the living God. Some people may pick up this book because they are struggling with childlessness themselves and are trying to understand their experiences in the light of their faith. Others – perhaps ministers, pastoral workers, those in positions of responsibility in churches – may be reading in order to understand the experience of childlessness better and to help support those who are going through it. All but the smallest congregations are likely to have members who wished for children and could not have them, or whose friends and family have had this experience.

Defining terms

In this book I consider the experience of involuntary childlessness: wanting to have children and being unable to do so. This includes, but is not limited to, the experience of infertility. The medical definition of infertility is failure to conceive after a year of unprotected sex. The vast majority of heterosexual couples, even where the female partner is in her late thirties, will conceive naturally within this timeframe. It is estimated that around 1 in 7 couples, or 15 per cent, will have difficulty conceiving.[2] Even when a couple do not achieve a pregnancy within a year, however, it is possible they will eventually conceive naturally, given time and perhaps outside help. Some struggle to conceive naturally but achieve a pregnancy following surgery, with the help of fertility drugs, or via assisted reproduction, such as in-vitro fertilization (IVF) or intra-uterine insemination (IUI). Not everyone who experiences infertility finds that it results in the permanent condition of childlessness.

Some couples find that they are able to conceive one child, but struggle to conceive more children. This is known as 'secondary infertility' and can be a source of deep pain, frustration and bitterness. During the course of researching this book I read and heard accounts of people who, despite having a child or children already, found their inability to conceive again intensely painful. Some people can become pregnant but have trouble staying pregnant, experiencing the agony of recurrent miscarriage and stillbirth. In addition to the difficulties experienced by heterosexual couples, single people and same-sex couples begin the quest to become parents at a considerable disadvantage. They have no option but to turn to assisted reproduction and/or adoption in order to have a child.

Some people who struggle with childlessness go on to adopt a child. It is very common for people experiencing infertility and childlessness to be told 'you can always adopt'. This comment is almost always unhelpful and reflects a lack of understanding of infertility, childlessness and adoption. First, infertility cannot be 'cured' by adoption. The inability to conceive a child carries shame and loss that cannot be erased. Kevin, an infertile adoptive parent, describes himself as a 'childless father' for this reason (Ellis 2013, pp. 130–1). Second, adoption cannot provide an infertile person with a child who shares their genes and resembles them or their partner. Third, in the UK, very few children are voluntarily relinquished and thus very few babies are available for adoption. Children in the care system are children who have experienced trauma, either in utero, in early childhood, or both, and have been removed from their parents once they have consistently shown themselves unable to provide adequate parenting. Becoming an adoptive parent means nurturing a child who has experienced losses that will have lifelong effects. Fourth, the process of being approved as an adopter and being matched with a child is long and gruelling. For all these reasons, adoption does not remove or reverse the pain of infertility and childlessness. It is an option that can only be explored when the childless person or couple has worked through the pain of their childlessness.

Although I write as a heterosexual married woman, within

the term 'people struggling with childlessness' I include both women and men, single people and couples, LGBT+ people and heterosexuals. The pain of childlessness is sometimes thought of as something experienced mainly by women, but this is not the case.[3] I have experienced infertility and childlessness as a woman with a male partner, but in describing my experience I am aware that many people within the LGBT+ community also long for children, and start this process with even more stacked against them biologically than I had. Furthermore, the sadness of being childless does not only affect those who are in relationships and might therefore be expected to have children. Single people also experience this sadness.[4] Finally, I am aware that people experiencing secondary infertility often experience the same grief, fury and struggle that I did. As I write, I have tried to hold in mind both women and men, couples and single people, gay and straight people, those with no children and those trying to expand their family. I do not want this book to compound the isolation experienced by all who struggle with childlessness by seeming to exclude some people from this experience.

This book is an extended reflection on the experience of those who are involuntarily childless. Some people who might have found themselves to be fertile choose not to have children, for a variety of reasons, and I would like to say from the outset that I respect this choice. They may be unsure of their ability to cope with a child; reluctant to pass on a genetic condition to a biological child; unwilling to contribute to the world's overpopulation. They may have careers or vocations that allow them to be creative and which would not be compatible with family life. I acknowledge that childlessness is not experienced by everyone as painful. The term 'childfree' has been coined as better reflecting the experience of people who make this positive choice; who do not feel that they lack anything by not having children. Nevertheless, it is not within the scope of this book to consider the experiences of those who choose childlessness. My concern is with the experience of those desperately wanting children and being unable to have them.

I have attempted to hold a wide variety of different experiences of involuntary childlessness in mind in my reflections, but there will be times when the filter of my own experience will cause me to miss aspects of others' experiences. I write from the UK context, where it is possible to have fertility treatment funded by the NHS. Readers in other countries will probably not have this privilege. As people's experiences of infertility and childlessness are so varied, not everything in this book will resonate with every reader. My hope is that there is something in each chapter that brings consolation to readers going through their own particular struggle with childlessness. Likewise, pastoral carers reading this book will need to bear in mind that not everything will be relevant to every person experiencing childlessness. People experience childlessness differently depending on all sorts of factors, such as their sexuality, gender, relationship status, physical health and family circumstances: not every experience touched on in this book will be common to all. I believe that the broad themes do apply to most people experiencing childlessness, however, including people who suffer recurrent miscarriage. I hope that everyone reading this who has had trouble having children will find some resonance, will recognize elements of their own story, and will experience healing.

Finally, I should explain that, for the most part, I will use 'me' and 'I' to describe my experience of infertility and childlessness. This is not to ignore the pain, anger and confusion my husband went through, just as intense and prolonged as my own. That is his story, however, and it is not mine to tell.

Notes

1 Phyllis Trible writes powerfully of this struggle with God. For her, it is a struggle to find the blessing in certain thorny 'texts of terror' in the Old Testament. See Trible 1992, pp. 1–5.

2 See 'Overview. Infertility', NHS, www.nhs.uk/conditions/infertility/, accessed 12.2.2018.

3 See, for example, the work of Robin Hadley at www.robinhadley.co.uk, and Kevin Ellis (2003, 2006, 2013).

4 See, for example, Jody Day (2016).

I

Alone

There are no meal trains organized by the [synagogue], no sympathy cards sent, no notices emailed to congregants: The Abramson's are saddened to announce the passing of the children they never got to have. Our loss is invisible and suffered in utter silence and isolation.[1]

The experience

People do not talk in fertility clinics. They do not even make eye contact. It was a counsellor who pointed this out to me. She worked with people being treated for cancer as well as those undergoing fertility treatment. The atmosphere in a cancer ward is very different from that in a fertility clinic, she explained. People with cancer talk to one another; they swap stories and tips; they keep one another's spirits up. In fertility clinics, no one speaks. As I sat in the counsellor's office, I could barely make eye contact with her. I was utterly defeated.

I do remember someone once catching my eye in a fertility clinic. It was a man, and I was furious with him. He and his partner were there with a baby. It was clear that they were undertaking another cycle of IVF to try and have a second child. Maybe they couldn't get a babysitter, my rational, adult internal voice suggested. But my inner child was raging. How could they be so insensitive? How could they have brought a baby into a fertility clinic? He caught my eye and he tried to smile. I think he was trying to encourage me – 'look, it works!' But I didn't want his encouragement: I wanted him and his partner and his baby to disappear.

By a strange coincidence, a few months after the unsuccessful end of my fertility treatment, I was able to observe the atmosphere in a cancer clinic for myself. I had to have surgery to remove a benign breast lump, which meant a few trips to the breast clinic. I was one of the lucky ones, but I was in a waiting room with women having treatment for breast cancer. I was in my late thirties, but looked younger. As they called my name and I got up, the older woman sitting next to me patted my arm and said, 'all the best – you'll be fine'. I was really touched.

I never had any desire to talk to anyone else in the waiting room of a fertility clinic, and I carefully avoided eye contact. I was so very unhappy, and so very angry with the world and everyone around me. If I spoke to the woman sitting next to me, I might find that she was younger than me, more fertile, with better odds, and that would only make me feel worse. No two people going through fertility treatment are alike, and I found the comparisons very painful. Others had more eggs, more embryos, even a child, and were coming back to increase the size of their family. Others complained of the side effects of the follicle stimulating hormones: I did not experience these side effects, for the simple reason that, even on the highest dose, I did not respond to the drugs. Some people had achieved a pregnancy but suffered the agony of miscarriage. I felt that they had suffered more, their hopes realized only to be cruelly dashed – what did I have to complain about? And yet, my grief remained. Those women's bodies could achieve a pregnancy, I told myself, whereas mine was then, and remains, barren. I did not want to swap stories. Sharing the pain sometimes increases it.

Infertility and childlessness can be extremely lonely. They trap a person in their own misery, driving a wedge between couples and separating childless people from others. Friends and family who have had no difficulty conceiving children may be hard to be around. Childless friends may quite understandably be unwilling to discuss their own childlessness. It can be very hard for a person struggling with childlessness to find a safe person to talk to. Childless couples have to negotiate difficult conversations, talking together about this huge issue in their lives and yet not talking too much or too often. The pain and the bitterness are exhausting, and they have to give each other a break from it. Then they have to decide who they will tell about their situation. The rigours of fertility treatment mean that a working person will almost certainly have to tell someone at work in order to get the time off they need for appointments. Some treatments, particularly IVF, are unpredictable and require both partners to have a day off at times that cannot be planned far in advance. But they will probably not want their treatment to become general knowledge. The pain of involuntary childlessness is so deep and the treatment so personal that those going through it will probably need a high degree of privacy to protect them from other people's unwelcome questions. They will not want to discuss their sex life or reproductive health with many people – if any at all. They probably will not want friends who are parents to explain how tired they are all the time and how having children isn't easy at all – and almost implying the childless person is lucky they don't have any.

The feelings of shame, inadequacy and bitterness that childlessness brings are difficult to talk about, and therefore profoundly isolating. Childlessness brings bitterness because having a baby is so easy for most people. Statistically, after a year of unprotected sex, 84 per cent of couples will conceive a child ('infertility' is therefore defined as failure to conceive after one year).[2] Some of those couples who don't conceive in the first year will, though, conceive in the second year; in other words, some will experience infertility, perhaps anxiety about their ability to conceive, only to find it happens naturally given time. Of course, it is well publicized that fertility declines with a woman's age, particularly after her mid-thirties. Nevertheless, the majority of couples will be able to conceive naturally even when the female partner is in her late thirties.[3] Knowing these statistics, failure to conceive after months and years of trying is very galling. All around, friends are falling pregnant with apparent ease; they decide they want another baby, and along it comes; they may have two or three children already, and another one comes along as a surprise. Seeing a woman pushing a double buggy with twins is especially painful: to an unhappily childless person, a woman with twins has hit the jackpot. They may worry as time goes on that they barely have time to conceive one child, let alone more, and yet they may not want their baby to be an only child. When you cannot conceive one child, or your pregnancies end in miscarriage, seeing someone with twins is like watching them eat a hearty meal while you are starving.

Some of the isolation of childlessness comes through others' inability to understand it. Brené Brown writes of the 'unintentional shame' that happens when people are uncomfortable with a topic, such as infertility and childlessness: 'Unintentional shame often happens when people are trying to be helpful but end up either giving unsolicited advice, judging or shutting down the conversation out of their own discomfort' (Brown 2007, p. 165). Talking about childlessness can be dangerous because childless people run the risk that their pain and struggle will be dismissed, denied, or met with judgement rather than acceptance and empathy. Sometimes people may seek to deny or minimize the pain by talking about the difficulties of raising children or the financial and social benefits of remaining childless. Often they will respond with a miracle baby story in the mistaken belief that this will be encouraging. Jody Day sees the 'miracle baby story' as a form of denial – of refusing to tolerate the discomfort of the possibility that their friend's childlessness may not be swept away with a miracle (Day 2016, p. 85). Sometimes advice may be given about an alternative treatment the person once read about in a magazine. In Christian circles, denial and minimization are likely to take the form of a declaration that 'God's timing is perfect', 'God is in control', or an exhortation to pray harder. While these statements may sound pious on the surface, in effect they seek to tidy away the pain by invoking God's plans and purposes. These platitudes can be used as a barrier which protects the hearer from having their beliefs about life and God challenged by someone else's pain. In episode 41 of the Ali Prato podcast *Infertile AF*, Karen explains that, while everyone in her family knew she was having intra-uterine insemination, no one talked about it.[4] Sometimes people are unwilling to have the conversation in the first place – it is just too awkward and uncomfortable.

Childlessness is more than a feminist issue, and yet the isolation that childless women feel may be compounded by their gender. Historically, childbearing has been seen as a vital part of what it means to be a woman, and this view of womanhood persists, causing great pain to women who cannot have children. Women's rights are enshrined in law and, in the affluent global north, almost all areas of work and experience are available to both women and men. Women are not, in theory, defined solely as baby-makers but as human beings who are able to pursue an education, climb a mountain, find stimulating work or start a family, or any combination of the above. More than at any other time in history, not having children should not be a source of shame to a woman – and yet, for so many, it is. Madelyn Cain describes this as the 'last great arena of feminism' – being able to be childless without having to justify one's state (Cain 2001, p. xvi). The notion that a woman's purpose in life is to have children has been profoundly challenged by the women's movement, and yet it seems to be so deeply ingrained that she should seek to reproduce. And when she cannot, the failure is very hard to bear. Jody Day's analysis of childlessness among women in the global north identifies the fetishization of motherhood, which declares that the only way for a woman to lead a meaningful life is through becoming a mother. It is not that a woman cannot seek meaning in other ways, but these are all seen as 'less than' the project of becoming the mother to a man's children. She sees this as pronatalist ideology founded on patriarchy. 'Pronatalism' or 'natalism' is the belief that people should reproduce, and consequent prejudice against people without children. Jody Day argues that this is a personal, social, economic, political and structural prejudice against people without children.[5] Some pronatalists are motivated by their Christian faith, in particular their readings of various Old Testament texts that seem to promote large families as a blessing from God and even a Christian duty (McKeown 2014). This is an ideology Day seeks to challenge in order to release childless women from the belief that their lives are over because they are not mothers (Day 2016, pp. 68f.).

Involuntary childlessness causes pain to both men and women, however, and I would not want to argue that a woman's pain is deeper or more devastating than a man's. Robin Hadley has researched the impact of childlessness on men's well-being, and found that men and women report similar levels of unhappiness and yearning around their childlessness.[6] In a video conversation created for World Childless Week 2020, four men, including Hadley, discuss the effect childlessness has had on them and on their relationships. Hadley explains that his desperation for children and anger about his situation consumed him in his mid-thirties. Sikhumbuzo Dube, a Christian pastor, describes the pain he feels every time he conducts a dedication service for a new baby in his congregation – a duty he cannot avoid and that triggers his grief. Andy Harrod explains that, while his wife cried, he felt angry, and yet feared upsetting his wife if he expressed this uncomfortable emotion. Michael Hughes shares a photograph of his visit to the grave of an ancestor, the first in a line of six 'Michael Hughes'. The visit brought home to him the crushing reality that he would be the last. He confesses that, two years later, it is still painful to look at the photograph. All four men describe the difficulty of communicating grief between partners, arguing that men are conditioned to express grief differently from women and may feel that they have to be strong and protect their partner from what they are feeling. The isolation childless people feel from those around them who are parents can thus be carried into their relationships, when each partner grieves differently and may not see each other's grief.[7]

People who cannot have children do not fit in. They are naturally excluded from the social networks that form organically at the NCT class and the school gate. There is no place for them on Mumsnet. Actually, this is not strictly true – there are threads on Mumsnet about 'trying to conceive' (abbreviated to 'TTC'). Once you have come to the realization that you will never achieve a BFP – Big Fat Positive, i.e. positive pregnancy test – there is no longer a place for you in the forum.[8] Some of the social isolation childless people experience can be self-imposed. They may withdraw from social situations that are painful, such as baby showers and christenings. They may avoid large social gatherings where they anticipate seeing lots of people with their children. I was once secretly glad to receive a wedding invitation that explicitly stated that no children could attend the reception. Unfortunately, when I got to the wedding breakfast, I discovered a number of breastfeeding mothers who could not, of course, leave their babies at home. The absence of toddlers and older children running around simply drew my attention to precisely those tiny children whose presence caused me the most visceral pain.

Social media can cause pain to people experiencing many different kinds of loss and struggle, including people who are involuntarily childless. 'Baby spam' can appear in your Facebook or Instagram feed at any time of day.[9] It has become axiomatic that we tend to post only edited, airbrushed highlights of our lives on our social media accounts. People post photographs of themselves on holiday with their family, or write about the cute and funny things their children have said. They are less likely to write about the sleepless nights, the tummy bugs, the existential angst they may feel despite being blessed with children. Here is an extract from my private journal, written five years ago when we had begun to realize that we were having trouble conceiving:

Checking my Facebook news feed is a risky business. I never know when I'll next be 'baby bombed'. Another picture of a newborn accompanied by 'may we introduce … to the world'. It's only natural, and I guess it's the quickest and easiest way of making the announcement – far quicker, easier and cheaper than sending out cards. But it means that the circle of those from whom I receive these announcements is wider. Friends from way back, friends of my younger brother, people younger, and in some cases far younger than me have become parents. It all adds to my panic. Every baby announcement that isn't ours seems to make ours less likely. Every successful conception, pregnancy and birth makes me wonder why my body isn't playing ball – whether it ever will.

I'm probably – definitely – over-sensitized, but I do struggle. I feel the same way about people's wedding photos. I made a decision not to use any of my wedding photos as my profile picture on Facebook because, frankly, I hadn't enjoyed looking at other people's beautiful wedding portraits back when I was single. It seemed a bit smug, just as the baby announcements seem smug. An unreasonable reaction perhaps, but feelings are feelings. They're not right or wrong, they just are ...

I'm sorry, Facebook friends, I wish I could rejoice in your baby joy. Maybe I would if I were a better person.

I have lost count of the number of people I have 'unfollowed' on social media once they posted a scan photo or a photo of their new baby or grandchild. This may seem trivial, and it certainly made me feel childish when I did it. But it really hurt, every time. My response was to isolate in order to protect myself from the pain – to 'unfollow' the person so that I would not see their posts and risk them triggering my sorrow.

The isolation is social, but it is also emotional. People experiencing childlessness often have to hide their true feelings, because there may not be a space where their feelings can be held. When there is a new baby, and everyone in your social circle is sending congratulations, but you cannot have children, you are in a tricky situation. The socially expected response is delight and joy, exclamation marks and smiley emojis. And yet, other people's baby news brings a range of emotions that are much less acceptable than joy. Sometimes your heart is breaking; at other times you just want to punch someone. How dare someone else experience such joy when you cannot? But there is no place for your grief or your anger, your cynicism or your bitterness, on a WhatsApp group with a new baby announcement. So, you do what you have to. You paste on a smile. You hide what you feel.

Both the social and the emotional isolation childless people experience are simply compounded in churches. Church communities tend to be more socially conservative than the general population, often with a very traditional view of marriage and family life. They will expect a couple to start having babies within a couple of years of marriage, and may start asking questions if the babies do not appear. Church programmes tend to follow the rhythm of the school year, with most if not all activities stopping over the school holidays. I have lost count of the number of times I have been told 'you can't hold that meeting then – it's half term'. Across all denominations, church attendees are older than the general population, and census data shows affiliation to the Christian faith is correlated with a person's age.[10] The younger you are, the less likely you are to call yourself a Christian and to attend church. Churches are aware of their fragility and of their declining congregations, and are so very desperate to 'bring in young families'. All this has the potential to marginalize childless people. The emotional isolation can be even worse. Anger at the fertile world or, even worse, at God – envy of others' children – these are not acceptable emotions for people who are meant to 'give thanks in all circumstances' (1 Thess. 5.18).

The consolation

What does a person of faith do with this experience of isolation? How can it be understood and how might it be overcome? Turning to the Scriptures, the person struggling with childlessness can find company; others who have shared their experience. The Old Testament in particular offers numerous examples of women (infertility is always a female problem in the Bible) who long desperately for a child for many years, in some cases becoming embittered as they watch sisters and rivals bearing child after child. Perhaps the first that springs to mind is the story of Hannah found in 1 Samuel 1:

> There was a certain man of Ramathaim, a Zuphite from the hill country of Ephraim, whose name was Elkanah son of Jeroham son of Elihu son of Tohu son of Zuph, an Ephraimite. He had two wives; the name of one was Hannah, and the name of the other Peninnah. Peninnah had children, but Hannah had no children.

Now this man used to go up year by year from his town to worship and to sacrifice to the LORD of hosts at Shiloh, where the two sons of Eli, Hophni and Phinehas, were priests of the LORD. On the day when Elkanah sacrificed, he would give portions to his wife Peninnah and to all her sons and daughters; but to Hannah he gave a double portion, because he loved her, though the LORD had closed her womb. Her rival used to provoke her severely, to irritate her, because the LORD had closed her womb. So it went on year after year; as often as she went up to the house of the LORD, she used to provoke her. Therefore Hannah wept and would not eat. Her husband Elkanah said to her, 'Hannah, why do you weep? Why do you not eat? Why is your heart sad? Am I not more to you than ten sons?' (1 Sam. 1.1–8)

For a person experiencing involuntary childlessness, surely comparison with others is one of the bitterest, most painful aspects of the journey. Some people have to endure open comparisons being made, perhaps if a sibling has produced children and the family are waiting for them to follow suit. Unspoken comparisons are all around, however. No matter how sensitive and diplomatic the person's family and friends, they are likely to see people all around them achieving easily and naturally what is, for them, proving so difficult. Of course, all the childless person sees is a couple with a baby and, unless they know the parents well, they probably have no idea how long the baby has taken to be conceived, and what difficulties there might have been. And yet the comparison hurts.

In the story from 1 Samuel 1, Peninnah is cruel in a way few people would consider acceptable today. She openly mocks Hannah for her childlessness, proudly displaying her many children. In this ancient polygamous family structure, Hannah not only suffers the indignity of being unable to give her husband children, but has to share him with another woman who has apparently had no difficulty in performing her wifely duty. The comparison would already be cruel without Peninnah's open taunting. And yet, when we consider the information we are given about the family dynamics, Peninnah's unkindness perhaps starts to make more sense. We are told that, while she and her children were each given a portion of the meat on the day of sacrifice, Hannah was given a double portion 'because [Elkanah] loved her, though the Lord had closed her womb' (1 Sam. 1.5). Hannah, it seems, despite failing to produce heirs for Elkanah, is his favourite. He loves her despite her childlessness; it seems that he loves her best. There are echoes of Rachel and Leah here, sisters both given in marriage to Jacob; Rachel the most loved, and Leah granted children in consolation for being second best (see Genesis 29). Elkanah seems to be hurt that his love is not enough for Hannah. 'Why is your heart sad? Am I not more to you than ten sons?' (1 Sam. 1.8). Relationships tested by a struggle with childlessness can become strained to breaking point, especially when emotionally, physically and financially demanding fertility treatment is involved. A BBC Radio 4 documentary explored the experiences of couples who eventually decided to stop fertility treatment. One couple described their decision to stop IVF when they realized that the treatment was taking too high a toll on them. The wife explained, 'I don't want a baby more than I want us.'[11] Hannah does not have a baby, but she is deeply loved. Of course, Hannah's story is not simply that of a happy marriage: it ends with the miracle of a baby boy. We will return to this later.

Hannah is remembered for her experience of infertility and its miraculous ending with a baby. Much more is told about the life of Abram's wife, Sarai, but she too is plagued by infertility:

Now Sarai, Abram's wife, bore him no children. She had an Egyptian slave-girl whose name was Hagar, and Sarai said to Abram, 'You see that the LORD has prevented me from bearing children; go in to my slave-girl; it may be that I shall obtain children by her.' And Abram listened to the voice of Sarai. So, after Abram had lived for ten years in the land of Canaan, Sarai, Abram's wife, took Hagar the Egyptian, her slave-girl, and gave her to her husband Abram as a wife. He went in to Hagar, and she conceived; and when she saw that she had conceived, she looked with contempt on her mistress.

Then Sarai said to Abram, 'May the wrong done to me be on you! I gave my slave-girl to your embrace, and when she saw that she had conceived, she looked on me with contempt. May the LORD judge between you and me!' But Abram said to Sarai, 'Your slave-girl is in your power; do to her as you please.' Then Sarai dealt harshly with her, and she ran away from her. (Gen. 16.1–6)

This is a really disturbing story, full of pain. First, there is the pain of Abram, unable to produce an heir in a culture where children were not only a sign of God's blessing – and infertility a sign of his curse – but necessary for continuing the family line and looking after the parents in old age. This was a culture of extended families where failure to produce offspring disrupted the whole social order. Then there is the fact that God has promised Abram offspring to outnumber the particles of dust on the earth and the stars in the sky yet, more than ten years on, no children have appeared and Abram and Sarai are even further past the age of childbearing. Sarai's anguish is perhaps of a slightly different kind. Abram needs an heir; Sarai is unable to fulfil her wifely duty and give him his heir. The Bible says nothing of male infertility – it is always apparently the woman who is 'barren'. Sarai so wants to give her husband a child that she offers him a surrogate: her slave-girl, Hagar. This is Sarai's initiative and yet, when Hagar does become pregnant, Sarai's jealousy and anger are terrible to behold, and she mistreats Hagar so badly that the young pregnant woman runs away. Finally, and most poignant, there is Hagar's pain. She is apparently given no choice in the matter at all, treated as a baby machine, impregnated by a man probably old enough to be her great-grandfather, and then punished for her youthful fertility.

Sarai's actions are morally repugnant, and yet I suspect many people struggling with infertility and childlessness will have some sympathy with her. Her husband has been told that he will have unnumbered offspring, and yet she has completely lost hope in her own body's ability to fulfil this promise. Like many people today who are denied the promise of a baby, she looks around in desperation for a way to make it happen, and alights upon her slave. There may be resonances here for people considering surrogacy today. In our time, surrogacy is usually a clinical procedure. A woman volunteers to be a host for an embryo where the biological mother cannot carry a child, or where the intended parents are gay men. In some cases, the surrogate may agree to be inseminated using the father's semen, and to hand over a child that is biologically hers to the childless couple. While surrogates sometimes stay in touch with the parents, there is no requirement to do so, and no sexual infidelity has taken place. To offer a young, fertile woman to your husband for sex makes it much more personal. Hagar can do naturally and easily what Sarai cannot. There is a sense in which she is more of a wife than Sarai, as she has provided Abram with the much-needed heir. Sarai's jealousy is perfectly natural and inevitable, as perhaps is Hagar's contempt. In her situation of enslavement, her ability to conceive a child is the only power she has over her mistress.

And yet, despite all this pain, there is also redemption here. Slave-girl though she may be, God has not forgotten Hagar. He sees her in the desert – *El Roi*, the God who sees (Gen. 16.13). Harshly, God tells her to go back to her mistress, but with words of consolation. God tells her that the child that has been conceived in her without reference to her wishes will himself become the father of a great nation (Gen. 16.9–12). She will be the mother of this nation – Hagar, the powerless slave-girl. To the modern mindset this may not seem much of a consolation; she is going back to a harsh life of servitude with a resentful mistress, and will eventually be thrown out of the house with her son to fend for themselves. Hers will not be a life of ease, but it will be a life of great significance.

There is redemption for Sarai and for Abram too. Fourteen more years go by – and, by this point, they must have been wondering if the promise would ever be fulfilled – and then, miraculously, Sarai, now called Sarah, becomes pregnant and gives birth to a son, Isaac. They wait an enormously long time for this wonderful blessing. Genesis tells us Abraham was 100, and Sarah 90, when Isaac was born. Whether we are to understand their ages as a literal statement of fact or an exaggeration for dramatic effect hardly matters; any couple who have waited 25 years to conceive must have long given up hope.

Doubtless many sermons have focused on Abram and Sarai's mistake in trying to hurry God up and make the promise happen in their own way. How often do Christians declare that 'God's timing is always perfect'? But as a person who has waited, and waited, and waited, until the possibility of pregnancy seems a pipe-dream, as likely as winning the Lottery, I empathize. In a situation over which you have so little control, the temptation is to do something, anything, to change it. *Maybe if I reduced my stress at work, I'd become pregnant? Maybe if I lost weight? Maybe we should try and find a way of hurrying the hospital up? Could we afford to go private? Would a private clinic keep us waiting for months and months and months while I got older and older, and then cancel the appointment at the last moment?* You want to do something, anything, to make it happen, and you worry that if you do not, it will pass you by. But you also know that there is little you can do to change things. Sarai and Abram do try and hurry things along, and their actions cause a lot of pain, not least for Hagar. And yet God promises great things for the baby who is born out of impatience, and he does not abandon Abram and Sarai in anger. Perhaps, if we pause at this point in the story, this is where we might find hope for those who are still living in disappointment. God sees. God does not forget. God sees the pain of a lowly slave-girl, who is treated like a thing without feelings or rights by everyone else. God looks at an infertile couple who are getting on in years and declares that the whole world will be blessed through them, even though their circumstances do not make that seem likely.

We have seen that people struggling with the pain of childlessness can find some company in the Scriptures. They can find tales of women and men who desperately want children but seem unable to have them. They can encounter jealous wives; triumphant rivals; couples who are getting on in years who have long given up hope of a child; desperate and tearful prayers; Sarai's cynical laughter. In addition to Abram and Sarai, Elkanah and Hannah and Jacob and Rachel, we find

Isaac and Rebekah, who initially had some trouble conceiving Jacob and Esau; Manoah and his wife, the parents of Samson; and Elizabeth and Zechariah, the parents of John the Baptist. There is, however, much that is alienating about these stories. Initially offering solace to people struggling with childlessness, these stories ultimately part company with them, because they always end with a miracle child. Kevin Ellis expresses this poignantly: 'Hannah pleads tearfully for children. How I wish sometimes that her prayers had not been answered. They would then resonate with my own' (Ellis 2003, p. 12).

Along with stories of infertility in the Bible, the stories we share today generally have a happy ending. A baby comes along after hope is gone: as a couple are about to start fertility treatment, or after it has failed, or once they have adopted a child. People are trying for years, give up trying, go on holiday, and then the woman discovers with surprise that she is pregnant. These kinds of stories warm the heart. They tell us that anything is possible; that what we so desperately want will come to us the moment we stop reaching out for it. These are great stories, but there are other stories too, ones that do not end with a baby, or that are still being played out. Kevin Ellis points out that, practically speaking, there is no infertility in the Bible, because stories of infertility always end with a miracle baby. The infertility is a literary device that heightens the miracle and underlines the significance of the (invariably male) child (Ellis 2006, pp. 9–11). This is a problem when searching in the Bible for companions on the lonely road of childlessness. Children are a sign of God's blessing in the Bible; infertility a sign of God's curse. Righteous people who are under this curse have their shame expunged by a miracle.

We have considered two stories that may have some resonances for people struggling with childlessness, but which are ultimately resolved with a miracle. If we are not blessed with a miracle ourselves, then we are still left with much pain and confusion with which these stories cannot help us. Let us now turn to a story from the time of the Old Testament Judges in which there is no apparent divine intervention:

In the days when the judges ruled, there was a famine in the land, and a certain man of Bethlehem in Judah went to live in the country of Moab, he and his wife and two sons. The name of the man was Elimelech and the name of his wife Naomi, and the names of his two sons were Mahlon and Chilion; they were Ephrathites from Bethlehem in Judah. They went into the country of Moab and remained there. But Elimelech, the husband of Naomi, died, and she was left with her two sons. These took Moabite wives; the name of one was Orpah and the name of the other Ruth. When they had lived there for about ten years, both Mahlon and Chilion also died, so that the woman was left without her two sons and her husband.

Then she started to return with her daughters-in-law from the country of Moab, for she had heard in the country of Moab that the LORD had had consideration for his people and given them food. So she set out from the place where she had been living, she and her two daughters-in-law, and they went on their way to go back to the land of Judah. But Naomi said to her two daughters-in-law, 'Go back each of you to your mother's house. May the LORD deal kindly with you, as you have dealt with the dead and with me. The LORD grant that you may find security, each of you in the house of your husband.' Then she kissed them, and they wept aloud. They said to her, 'No, we will return with you to your people.' But Naomi said, 'Turn back, my daughters, why will you go with me? Do I still have sons in my womb that they may become your husbands? Turn back, my daughters, go your way, for I am too old to have a husband. Even if I thought there was hope for me, even if I should have a husband tonight and bear sons, would you then wait until they were grown? Would you then refrain from marrying? No, my daughters, it has been far more bitter for me than for you, because the hand of the LORD has turned against me.' Then they wept aloud again. Orpah kissed her mother-in-law, but Ruth clung to her. (Ruth 1.1–14)

Naomi has been fertile – she has been blessed with two sons – but her sons have both died young, before fathering children.

Her husband, Elimelech, has also died. Her life started out promising and yet all that early hope has ended in despair. She knows that she is too old to remarry or to have more children. She is understandably bitter and feels that she is under God's curse.

Orpah and Ruth share in Naomi's tragedy, having lost their husbands. It seems they are still young enough to marry again, however, so Naomi urges her daughters-in-law to go and seek new husbands so that they may have happier lives than she has had. Orpah loves her mother-in-law, but does what she suggests, parting tearfully. Ruth, however, refuses to leave Naomi's side. Ruth's love for her mother-in-law and her loyalty to her are deeply touching. Naomi has lost her sons, but has a daughter who will not leave her even for her own self-interest. Ruth insists on sharing Naomi's struggle rather than returning to her birth family – which would presumably have been easier, in a culture in which women depended entirely on men for their keep.

These women stick together, and come up with a plan for improving their lot. They seek out a relative of Naomi's late husband, a man called Boaz, who might be prevailed upon to restore the family fortunes by marrying Ruth, continuing Elimelech's line and securing the women's future. It is Ruth's idea that she should go and glean in Boaz's field (Ruth 2.2), collecting up the grain left by those who are harvesting, an accepted means of providing for the poor at that time and in that culture. Once Ruth has attracted Boaz's interest and protection, Naomi figures out what she should do next (Ruth 3.1–4). Ruth carries out Naomi's audacious plan, going to find Boaz once he is full of good food and wine, uncovering him while he sleeps, and lying down beside him. Boaz is startled – it seems that there is some potential risk to Ruth's reputation, as he does not want anyone else to see that she came to the threshing-floor (Ruth 3.14). Audacious though the plan may have been, nevertheless Boaz is an honourable man, and assures Ruth that he will do right by her. The women's assertiveness pays off: Boaz agrees to act as 'kinsman-redeemer', marries Ruth, and restores the family's fortunes. Ruth gives birth to Obed and Naomi is overjoyed. At the end of the story, 'the women of the neighbourhood' declare that Ruth, a woman related only by marriage, is 'more to Naomi than seven sons'. Furthermore, Ruth's son is seen as, in a sense, Naomi's child too. Through Ruth, Naomi has hope and a future once again.

Sarai, Abram and Hagar experience much grief when Sarai and Abram take matters into their own hands to bring forth the long-awaited child. Naomi and Ruth take positive action and experience great joy as a result, however. Two very unfortunate and vulnerable women are able to turn their lives around. There is much that people struggling with childlessness can do in twenty-first-century Britain to make their dream come true. While the funding of fertility treatment varies greatly between clinical commissioning groups, nevertheless many people can have fertility treatment on the NHS. In the story of Ruth and Naomi, God's blessing comes through their own actions to improve their lot – actions borne not just out of self-interest but out of their love for each other. People who embark upon fertility treatment can find company here in this story of two women who are able to make a bright future for themselves.

Where is the grace for those of us who find that, ultimately, nothing we do is able to make the dream happen? I think it is found in the closing verses of Ruth. Through Naomi's tragedy, she finds a loving and faithful daughter in the wife of her dead son, and a grandson who is no blood relative. Granted, there is a particular set of customs in operation here, whereby a male relative could marry a man's widow and produce heirs to continue the dead man's family line. Nevertheless, this is a powerful story for those of us whose lives do not turn out the way we wanted them to – the way other people's lives seem to turn out. Those of us who do not find a life partner, or who are not able to have children with our partner, can find hope in this story. Family is determined not just by biology, but by those whom we choose to love. We will return to the story of Ruth in Chapter 6, where we will consider its use in preaching.

Finally, we turn to a story in which a woman's shame and isolation are overcome by the mercy of Jesus. In Mark and Luke we read about Jesus' encounter with a woman who was probably infertile:

> As [Jesus] went, the crowds pressed in on him. Now there was a woman who had been suffering from haemorrhages for twelve years; and though she had spent all she had on physicians, no one could cure her. She came up behind him and touched the fringe of his clothes, and immediately her haemorrhage stopped. Then Jesus asked, 'Who touched me?' When all denied it, Peter said, 'Master, the crowds surround you and press in on you.' But Jesus said, 'Someone touched me; for I noticed that power had gone out from me.' When the woman saw that she could not remain hidden, she came trembling; and falling down before him, she declared in the presence of all the people why she had touched him, and how she had been immediately healed. He said to her, 'Daughter, your faith has made you well; go in peace.' (Luke 8.42b–48; see also Mark 5.25–34)

As a woman experiencing infertility and childlessness, I find this passage offers deep consolation. The unnamed woman has been 'suffering from haemorrhages' for 12 years. We have no way of knowing what exactly was wrong with her, although we can make some educated guesses, but the precise details hardly matter. We are told that she had 'spent all she had' on doctors and yet had found no cure. Treatments for infertility can be very, very expensive. Women and men reading this passage who are struggling with childlessness may also be in the position of having suffered for years; having spent all they have and still not been able to have a child. The 'postcode lottery' in the UK regarding funding for fertility treatment has been well publicized. The National Institute for Health and Care Excellence recommends that three fresh cycles of IVF be offered to infertile couples in order to give the treatment the optimum chance of success. While a few health authorities will fund the full three cycles, most fund just two, just one, or none at all.[12] An article published on the BBC website on 30 October 2017 revealed that, of the 208 clinical commissioning groups in England, only 24 offered three cycles of IVF to infertile couples, and seven offered none at all.[13] Within a year of finishing our IVF treatment, we discovered that our own clinical commissioning group had taken the decision to reduce the number of funded cycles from two to just one, and only for women under 40. This inequality leaves individuals and couples – depending on where they live – in the position of having to find thousands of pounds for each cycle they undertake, putting them under considerable financial pressure, and excluding the poorest and those without access to credit entirely. And those who do end up paying for their own treatment may bear a huge emotional and physical cost, as well as a financial one, and yet end up with no child at the end of their treatment. There are resonances here with the position of the woman who reached out to touch the cloak of Jesus.

We do not know how old this woman was, and whether she already had children. Perhaps she had developed this debilitating condition after giving birth. It is entirely possible, however, that she had suffered in this way since puberty, in which case she is unlikely to have married and it seems highly unlikely that she will have been able to produce children. Many modern readers of the Bible are familiar with the Jewish purity laws which dictated that certain people were ritually 'unclean'. A menstruating woman would not have been able to go to the temple, and were she to touch anyone during her menstruation she would make them unclean too. As she was always menstruating, the woman in this story would have suffered terrible isolation. She epitomizes what it is to live in shame. She was 'bad' from the inside out, unfit to touch others, let alone to come before God, ostracized from her community – and all because of something over which she had no control. Any woman who has gone through the monthly ritual of trying to time her ovulation, having regular sex with her partner at her most fertile time of the month, the early pregnancy test and bitter disappointment, will understand the frustration of having no control over her own body. How fervently this nameless woman has tried to cure herself of her affliction, using all the money she had to pay for medical care, to no avail. And this desperate woman has dared to stretch out her hand and touch someone, and a holy man at that. Despite her ostracism, her years of shame, she still has enough faith and enough hope to reach for the fringe of Jesus' cloak.

The Bible tells us that her haemorrhage stops immediately – she is miraculously healed – and yet surely this is not the most wonderful part of the story. Jesus knows that healing power has gone out from him, and perhaps knows exactly what has happened, but he insists on talking with the person who has been healed. 'Who touched me?' he asks. Courageous though the woman has already been in reaching out in faith for her healing, surely coming before Jesus to own up to what she has done takes even more courage. This shamed, untouchable woman, whose condition is so mortifying, has to admit to Jesus why she touched him. She has to allow herself to be seen. And yet, far from rebuking her, Jesus speaks the words that complete her healing: 'Daughter, your faith has made you well; go in peace' (Luke 8.48). He commends the faith she has shown in reaching out to God, through him, to ask for divine healing. Far from condemning her, Jesus praises her. 'Go in peace.' Her healing is as emotional and psychological as it is physical. She is accepted. She is enough. She is a woman of faith, loved by God.

Perhaps there is hope here for those who are still in the middle of the infertility struggle; whose story has not, or not yet, ended with a baby. We do not know anything about what happened to this woman after her encounter with Jesus. She lived in a society where a woman's only protection was marriage and her chief duty to produce children. If, as seems quite likely, she was unmarried and childless, we do not know that her state changed. She may by this point have been considered too old for marriage, bearing in mind that life expectancy in first-century Palestine was much lower than it is for us. Those of us who have not yet had our miracle baby, or who have resigned ourselves to the knowledge that this baby will never come, might see ourselves in this woman. Through her story we may be able to grasp the possibility of a healing of mind and spirit that comes by being acceptable to a Lord who knows, who cares, who will not allow us to stay in the shadows, defined by our shame. Jesus has seen her in all her 'uncleanness' and has declared her fit to be seen, to be touched, to be blessed by God. She is acceptable. She is made whole.

The practice

We have – finally – found company and consolation in the Bible, and this is no small thing. People struggling with child-lessness need to find company in the Scriptures. They also need the company of other human beings. What liberative praxis might overcome the isolation of involuntarily childless people?

On the first Mothering Sunday after we were told there was no point continuing with fertility treatment, I got a knock at the door. My friend M was there, asking if she could come in for a chat. Suddenly her two children, then five and seven years old, jumped out from around the corner of the house yelling 'surprise!' and holding out a bunch of flowers, a box of my favourite chocolates and some home-made Mother's Day cards. M told me later that she had explained to them that it would be nice to make some cards for Emma, because she didn't have any children. 'Yes she does!' the youngest one declared, 'she's got us!'

What M and her children did for me was very risky indeed. To make a Mother's Day card for a woman who has just dis-covered she will never be a biological mother. To knock on her door on the very day that can be most painful for women struggling with childlessness. To declare that she does have children who love her, albeit someone else's children, who will always love their own mother best. To defy the sorrow and the grief with the gift of cards made with love. This was a very powerful statement, and it could have backfired badly. M later told me that she had been unsure about telling me the 'she's got us' comment, for fear that it would upset me – but she decided to take a risk and tell me anyway. All of this could have triggered grief and pain. Doubtless it would have triggered grief and pain for some women. It did not trigger pain for me, and I will never forget it.

The popular shame researcher and writer Brené Brown argues for the importance of showing vulnerability and seeking connection in order to develop what she terms 'shame resilience'. During the Q&A after a talk given at the Royal Society for Arts, Manufactures and Commerce in 2013, Brown was asked specifically about the experience of childless women who find that, when they are vulnerable and share their pain, it is dismissed or minimized, for example by a miracle baby story.[14] Brené Brown explained that her research had found infertility to be one of the principal areas of 'empathy failure' – one of the areas of human experience that seemed to be most shrouded in shame. She advised that people experiencing childlessness take the risk of writing a letter asking for what they need. In her first book, *I thought it was just me*, she quotes extensively from an open letter by Jody Earle, who struggled with infertility for 11 years. In the letter, Earle explains what she is going through, what is unhelpful, and what she needs from her friends (Brown 2007, pp. 165f.). This is an act of great courage, and not something I would have found it at all easy to do when my grief was at its most raw. Perhaps in the context of pastoral counselling, however, people struggling with childlessness might be encouraged to express what they need – both to those caring for them pastorally and to their friends and family. If I had written such a letter, it might have said something like this:

> I can't have biological children, and the long journey I have taken to come to this realization is the worst thing that's ever happened to me. I feel angry most of the time, especially when I'm reminded that other people find it easy to have their own children. This feels painfully unfair and the bitterness is hard to live with. What makes it worse is that there's absolutely nothing I can do to change my situation. I've done all that can be done and now my husband and I have to grieve and heal.

Please don't tell me that God's in control, or that God's timing is perfect. When you say that, it sounds as if you're telling me to be quiet and put up with it. It also makes me doubt whether the God you believe in loves me at all, because of the pain I'm in. Please don't tell me that God will answer my prayers, 'just not in the way I expect'. That makes a mockery of the prayers I've prayed. It makes me feel like God isn't really listening. Please don't remind me of the benefits of not having children, or tell me I can 'just adopt'. Telling me about sleepless nights and cluttered homes doesn't make my pain go away. And as for 'just adopt' – do you have any idea how long and painful the adoption process is?

What would really help me is if you would listen, and not try to make me feel better. I know it's instinctive to want to take away the pain, but you can't. I know it may make you feel uncomfortable to be around someone who is feeling this unhappy. But if you can love me enough to be with me in my pain, you will really help me. And if you want to help me understand what God is saying through my experiences, ask me questions. Help me figure it out for myself. Don't tell me what you think are the right answers. The answers don't make sense any more. I need a new set of answers.

At their best, churches can be places that transcend the nuclear family. In the 17 years since I first joined a church, I have sometimes been invited into other people's families in profoundly healing ways. For the first seven years, I attended church as a single woman, and yet I had friends who invited me to hang out with their families, to become part of their children's lives. This happened again when I was married and childless. There was a woman around my age who came to me for pastoral counselling. Just a few weeks later, I was signed off work with stress. No one in the church at that time knew the reason: that I had finally been referred for IVF treatment and was miserable. Disappointed that my reprieve had not come; anxious about the treatment – both the physical demands it would place on my body and the ethical dilemmas with which it would force us to engage. The woman who had trusted me in her vulnerability now ministered to me in mine. Her youngest child was a pre-schooler at that time, and she often invited me round for meals during the day, as neither of us was at work. Several weeks later, I returned to work, and stopped popping round to visit her during the day. She later told me that her son found this a little confusing, asking where Emma's place at the table was. For him, I had become part of the furniture. My husband and I have since got to know the family well, often babysitting the children and never feeling 'less than' because of our childless state.

One of the problems with grief is the awkwardness we all feel, not knowing what to say. The sad fact is that many of us say nothing. I would argue that nothing is never the right thing to say. Better to say something and get it wrong than to say nothing at all. When we make an effort and take a risk, we show the person that we love them enough to take that chance. We show them that they are not alone. We overcome their isolation.

American artist Emily McDowell has created a series of empathy cards. Her website features this strapline: 'Empathy: What to say, when you don't know what to say'. Her range of empathy cards feature a contemporary design and include the following options, in each case printed on the front of the card:

In case you'd like infertility to be even more devastating, there's good news: the general public is also on hand to judge your choices!
[In smaller letters]: I'm so sorry you're going through this

The five stages of grief: crying in public, crying in the car, crying alone while watching TV, crying at work, crying while you're a little drunk
[In smaller letters]: I love you

There is no good card for this. I'm so sorry.

Well, this just sucks. I wish I had a better way to say it, but my brain feels totally stuck right now. But I just want you to

know that even though I might not always have exactly the right words, you will always have me. I'm not going anywhere. So I hope you're cool with that.
[In tiny letters]: because I love you.[15]

There is much that is so helpful in these cards. Acknowledging suffering and not denying the pain it brings. Gentle humour that eases the social awkwardness of trying to comfort someone for whom no comfort is adequate. A down-to-earth rather than philosophical approach. Most importantly, however, these cards declare solidarity with the person in pain, letting them know that they are not alone. The cards seem to be particularly designed for situations when most of us don't know what to say, so many of us say nothing at all. And yet they promise company on the journey: 'even though I might not always have exactly the right words, you will always have me. I'm not going anywhere.'

Moving from the practice of individual Christians to the corporate life of a Christian community, what can be done to overcome the marginalization and isolation of people struggling with childlessness? Few if any churches would teach explicitly that married people with children are more welcome than others in the life of the Church, and yet this can be the unintentional impression that is given in a thousand small ways. Churches often seem to be designed around the nuclear family and, as a result, single people and childless couples can struggle to know where they fit. Job pages are filled with advertisements for children and families workers, as churches nurture their obsession with 'bringing in young families'. Churches want to feel vital and alive, with younger people to do the jobs that need doing; to contribute to the offering; to raise the 'church of the future'. They are haunted by the memory of full churches bursting with children in times gone by. A significant proportion of church activities are aimed at children and families, with toddler groups, youth groups, Messy Church and Sunday school all being regular parts of many church programmes. Many churches have a pre-school that meets on its premises, providing childcare for very small children. All-age services can, if not done well, feel more like kids' services with adults as spectators.

Two services that can highlight this nuclear family focus in potentially alienating ways are infant baptisms and Mothering Sunday. In my own Baptist tradition, babies are not baptized but instead are brought forward for 'dedication', usually during a normal Sunday morning service. The parents make promises to love and care for the child, and to share their faith with him or her. The congregation promise to help the parents. Finally, some words of blessing are said over the baby. It is natural that parents come with a sense of joy, wanting to give thanks to God for the gift of the child. This can be a very difficult service for those of us who have been denied this gift, however. Mothering Sunday is a pastoral minefield for all sorts of reasons. In addition to those grieving their childlessness, there will be people whose mothers have died; people who are estranged from their adult children; people whose relationships with their mothers are complex and strained. Good pastoral practice foresees many of these potential pitfalls and is sensitive to them. I have worshipped in churches where all women over 18 received a Mothering Sunday gift and where pastoral prayers during the service recognized the complex mix of emotions some people would be feeling.

Having said all this, I believe one of the strengths of churches is the way in which the generations mix in ways they do not in other walks of life. The welcoming of children and young people and the provision of activities suitable for all ages is surely to be encouraged. The trick is, I think, to welcome children and young people in such a way that people without children do not feel they are excluded. In the dedication services I have conducted, there has generally been a point where I have turned to the congregation and asked, as part of the liturgy, whether they would commit to support the family with love and prayers and to share their faith with the child. The Baptist prayer book *Gathering for Worship* suggests that the question be put to the congregation in this way:

Gathered here as members of this congregation
and as representatives of the wider Church of God
do you promise to offer A and *her/his* family
your love and support,
and, being faithful in prayer,
will you share your faith with *her/him*
by word and example?
If you will promise this, please stand ...
(Ellis and Blyth 2005, p. 54)

A similar question is asked at weddings, inviting the congregation to promise to care for and pray for the newly married couple, and to support them in their relationship. These are simple ways in which the role of the whole congregation, transcending the nuclear family unit, can be affirmed.

Going beyond these simple liturgical affirmations of the role of the church family, preachers could take the opportunity of an infant baptism or dedication, Mothering Sunday or Father's Day service to preach on the role of the wider church community. This passage from Matthew 12 could be taken as a text:

> While he was still speaking to the crowds, his mother and his brothers were standing outside, wanting to speak to him. Someone told him, 'Look, your mother and your brothers are standing outside, wanting to speak to you.' But to the one who had told him this, Jesus replied, 'Who is my mother, and who are my brothers?' And pointing to his disciples, he said, 'Here are my mother and my brothers! For whoever does the will of my Father in heaven is my brother and sister and mother.' (Matt. 12.46–50; see also Mark 3.31–35; Luke 8.19–21)

What does it mean to be the body of Christ – a loving community that transcends the nuclear family? How might our understanding of 'family' grow to include single and childless people? These questions could be explored in preaching at appropriate moments in the church year, asserting a view of family that goes beyond two parents and their biological children in discrete family units.

Another very simple way of overcoming the isolation of people struggling with childlessness is for church leaders to talk about childlessness openly, 'from the front'. This is difficult for all sorts of reasons. People do not generally feel comfortable discussing their experiences of childlessness in public. And yet, this is part of the problem: the conspiracy of silence, driven in part by shame. In Chapter 6 I make suggestions for preaching that engages with pain, struggle and confusion in general, and childlessness in particular. This is one simple way of beginning to overcome the isolation of childless people: tackling the issue head on. Naming the pain and the shame of childlessness. Not shying away from stories like that found in Genesis 30, where Rachel says to Jacob, 'Give me children, or I shall die!' (30.1). Acknowledging that these are the raw depths to which childlessness can send a person. Resisting the temptation to tidy up by pointing out Rachel's happy ending, for which, surely, she should have trusted God all along. Or by suggesting that Rachel had inappropriately made children an idol. Choosing to stay with the pain and thus making a place for it in public discourse. Refusing to let childlessness stay in the shadows, keeping people silent and shamed.

It is common practice for people to be introduced on the church website or at a Christian conference with a brief biography, mentioning the name of their spouse and the number of children they have. This practice can be profoundly alienating for people who are single, or married without children. I would strongly encourage editors of church websites and speakers at conferences to avoid offering the kinds of biographical details that marginalize others.

Truly liberative practice would, I believe, see people from a greater diversity of family circumstances in Christian leadership. We need single and childless ministers and church leaders as well as those who are married with children. When those who are leading worship, delivering sermons and devising church programmes all come from one particular demographic, it is inevitable that churches will come to resemble the people who lead them. In my late twenties I served as a lay worker alongside a couple who were open about their childlessness. The husband was an associate minister and his wife had a consider-able pastoral and musical ministry. At the time, I was single and exploring a call to Christian ministry. All the ministers I knew were married with children. It was very helpful to me to see people in ministry whose lives, like mine, looked a little different. When a greater diversity of life experience is repre-sented 'from the front', a greater diversity of life experiences 'in the pews' will be accepted.

Notes

1 Ruth Levy Abramson, an Orthodox Jewish woman living in Israel, quoted in Day 2016, p. 103.

2 'Overview. Infertility', *NHS*, www.nhs.uk/conditions/infertility/, accessed 12.2.2018.

3 Jean M. Twenge has conducted a helpful analysis of fertility stat-istics for women over 35. She cites a study that found that 82 per cent of couples having regular unprotected sex, where the female partner was aged 35 to 39, got pregnant in a year, rising to 90 per cent after two years. See Twenge 2012, pp. 111–12.

4 Ali Prato, *Infertile AF*, https://infertileaf.libsyn.com

5 Bibi Lynch, 2020, 'Being Childless: Grief and Acceptance', *MyPoint. tv*, 6 September, https://mypoint.tv/news/world/f3a5665c-f11f-11ea-83 a5-oeaa513b9aa1?utm_sq=giw9d11fpi&fbclid=IwAR3sSEJTFgoV cMPzAI3yGmmosp-U307Xi10O3-DcQU9x0CXPLqTesV9MK9M, accessed 17.1.2021.

6 Robin Hadley, 'Frequently Asked Questions', *Robin Hadley*, www.robinhadley.co.uk/frequently-asked-questions/, accessed 17.1. 2021.

7 Sikhumbuzo Dube, Robin Hadley, Andy Harrod and Michael Hughes, 2020, '4 guys from 3 continents', *World Childlessness Week*, 17 September, https://worldchildlessweek.net/thurs-17-2020/4-guys-from-3-continents, accessed 17.1.2021.

8 See www.mumsnet.com

9 I have borrowed this hilarious phrase from Lizzie Lowrie (2020), p. 157.

10 Ami Sedghi, 2013, 'UK Census: religion by age, ethnicity and country of birth', *The Guardian*, 16 May, www.theguardian.com/news/datablog/2013/may/16/uk-census-religion-age-ethnicity-coun try-of-birth, accessed 7.3.2021.

11 *Drawing the Line: When IVF Doesn't Work*, first broadcast on 29 May 2015 on BBC Radio 4.

12 Winston 2015, chapter 1. Winston points out the cruelty of this policy, asking what other medical treatment would be abandoned half-way through, before it has had a good chance of working?

13 'IVF: Patients face postcode lottery for treatment', *BBC News*, 30 October 2017, www.bbc.co.uk/news/uk-england-41764665, accessed 5.3.2018. NICE recommends that three cycles of IVF be offered to couples who have been trying unsuccessfully to conceive for at least two years, where the woman is under 40.

14 RSA, 2013, 'RSA Replay – The Power of Vulnerability', *YouTube*, broadcast live 4 July 2013, www.youtube.com/watch?v=QMzBv35H bLk

15 See https://emilymcdowell.com/collections/empathy-cards, accessed 7.3.21.

2

In Pain

A woman is screaming and screaming. There is running in the corridor and some porters come and drag her away. She has had three goes and they have told her nothing more can be done. All the day I can hear her still screaming and screaming. (Walton 2003, p. 207)

The experience

I remember exactly where I was when I got the phone call that effectively ended my hopes of having a baby. I was at work, and alone in my office at the church where I was a minister. It was our second round of IVF, and it was not going well. We had just one egg, and it had fertilized; we were hoping for an embryo transfer in a couple of days' time. The clinic called me to explain that our one embryo – our last embryo – was not developing well, and that they might not be able to use it. I had injected over £2,000 worth of medication into my abdomen in the previous two weeks, to little effect. We had reached the end of our funding and the end, it seemed, of what my body was able to accomplish. In the end, they did transfer the embryo and, as expected, it did not implant: I did not conceive.

A few weeks later we had a follow-up appointment at the fertility clinic. Our consultant had since moved on, so we were seen by a doctor who did not know us and had not read our notes. We sat in her office while she struggled with the computer, which was apparently refusing to divulge our treatment details. While she clicked the mouse impatiently, I started summarizing our treatment myself: it seemed quicker. I do not remember anything she said except for one phrase: 'there is no clinical reason to continue'. It was said with compassion, but utter finality. Game over.

Infertility and childlessness bring many different kinds of pain. For a woman, there is physical pain. The stomach cramps that announce the arrival of a period and the death of another hope. The cramping that comes with some diagnostic tests, such as when liquid is pumped through the fallopian tubes so that an X-ray image can be taken. The sharp pain of a needle inserted repeatedly into the ovaries in the hope of finding eggs. The agonizing pain of miscarriage: the body wracked with labour pains that do not joyfully end with a baby.[1]

For women and men there is emotional pain. There is the acute distress brought on by bad news delivered by a consultant; by a friend's announcement that she is pregnant; by a negative pregnancy test. There is also a chronic pain that must be endured: a long-running, low-level, nagging pain which goes on for months and years as the negative pregnancy tests and the failed treatments pile up. It is a pain that never quite goes away, and that can resurface unexpectedly. A baby cries in a supermarket and his cries of rage and frustration echo your own: cries to which you may never have given voice. A new baby is born to a friend or family member, and the hard-won peace and acceptance seem to be swept away on a fresh tidal wave of pain. The pain ebbs and it flows, there are crises and there are times of respite, but without the miracle baby it never really goes away. Elaine Tyler May's respondents express this powerfully:

> Struggling with childlessness is a death that you never fully mourn, a dream that never dies, a hope that never fades ... infertility has changed me ... There is not a part of my life or those who love me that have not been affected by this.
>
> I literally was going out of my mind with grief and disappointment. (Tyler May 1995, pp. 224, 15)

The emotional pain of childlessness is grief, and it needs to be recognized as such. People struggling with childlessness, their friends and families, and their churches, need to understand that a person trying to come to terms with their inability to have children is grieving – that they need to grieve, in order to heal. And yet, the grief of childlessness is unlike other griefs. With the exception of the agonizing tragedy of stillbirth, there is no body; no funeral; no public acknowledgement that there is a gap in the world. And yet there is loss. So much loss. This loss has to be mourned. A counsellor told us that we had experienced three bereavements: three embryos transferred that did not become babies. Three microscopic blobs of human possibility that did not fulfil their potential. My gametes mixed with my husband's and did produce the beginnings of life, but that life ended before it really began. There was something extremely intimate, it seemed to me, in knowing that we had become even more profoundly one flesh: a kind of final consummation; his flesh and mine joined to make an embryo. And yet, those embryos never became babies. I have read that some people think of those lost embryos as babies that never were; even give them names. An embryo that fails to implant is in a sense a very early miscarriage.[2]

It did not seem that way to me, however. I mourned, not those three specific embryos, but the hypothetical children we would never have. Like many people, I already knew the baby names I liked. I imagined the wonder of seeing my body change. I wanted to breastfeed a baby, to hold a tiny bundle of life in my arms, to fill our large, empty house with children. My grief was knowing that those things would never happen. I had friends whose close family members had died, and my loss seemed insignificant compared with theirs. They mourned a living, breathing person they had known and loved and lost. I mourned people I had never met. Children who had never been born; who never would be born. Although my grief was more abstract, it was very real, and I had to feel it, to come to terms with it, to learn to live with it. That took time. More time than I expected.

The grief of childlessness, like other griefs, is expressed in diverse ways. In her groundbreaking book *On Death and Dying* Elisabeth Kübler-Ross identified denial, anger, bargaining and depression as ways in which the pain of grief shows itself, sometimes ultimately ending in acceptance as the person comes to terms with their loss (Kübler-Ross 1969). This has come to be known as the 'grief cycle' and yet, in *On Grief and Grieving*, she and David Kessler explain that this was never intended to be understood as a predictable linear process. Not everyone experiences all these 'stages', and yet they are aspects of the way in which grief manifests itself that can be helpful to notice as we seek to cope with our own and others' grief.

For people struggling with childlessness, denial could show itself as the refusal to accept a diagnosis, or perhaps an insistence on carrying on after the failure of the umpteenth treatment cycle. In her study of people dying in hospital, Kübler-Ross observed that some fought their illness to the end, and that this fighting spirit was often affirmed by medical staff and by the dying patient's family, who saw 'giving up' as cowardly, as a rejection of those left behind. Kübler-Ross argued that this refusal to give up made it impossible for those dying to accept their death and to die in peace (Kübler-Ross 1969, p. 125). Not everyone who struggles with childlessness will have a baby, and there comes a point when accepting defeat is necessary in order to grieve and achieve a state of peace. It is of course down to the individual or couple to determine when it is right to give up and accept defeat. To have people suggest alternative treatments, urging a person to carry on the struggle, when they are at their limit and want to stop, is unhelpful. Kübler-Ross tells the story of Mrs W, whose husband and doctors insisted on fresh surgery when she had reached acceptance and wanted to die in peace. It was not until a psychotic episode as she was being prepared for surgery that her doctors and her husband understood that, while they wanted her to carry on, Mrs W wanted a peaceful death (Kübler-Ross 1969, pp. 125f.). It may sound over-dramatic to those unfamiliar with the experience to compare involuntary childlessness with a person dying in hospital. Childlessness, however, is the death of a hope; the death of a possible future; the death of all the potential children who will never be. It is intensely painful. As heartbreaking as it is, there comes a point when the hope of a child has to be allowed to die. Jody Day expresses this poignantly:

... over the years, whenever I'd tried to talk about my fears about not becoming a mother, all I'd ever been told was, 'Don't give up hope ... I heard this story ...' (you know the ones). And so I hadn't. And yet still, there I was. What I didn't yet understand was that giving up hope is actually really important. It's the first (utterly excruciating) step to coming to terms with childlessness. (Day 2016, pp. 5–6)

The bargaining associated with grief could perhaps manifest as constant obsessing over 'what ifs'. What if we'd started trying straight away? What if I'd gone to the doctor sooner? What if a different drug regimen had been tried? These 'what ifs' are fruitless, but can be a useful distraction from the pain of childlessness (Kübler-Ross and Kessler 2005, p. 19).[3] It may be helpful for people coming to terms with their childlessness to understand that this kind of thinking is a common feature of grief. This might help them not to take these thoughts too seriously, but to accept them and to let them go.

Anger is a significant part of the grief journey, and this was the emotion I experienced most often as I grieved my childlessness. Elaine Tyler May describes the 'almost bottomless rage' her respondents felt: anger directed at their own uncooperative bodies, and at the fertile world (Tyler May 1995, p. 225). Anger is an aspect of grief that can be particularly hard for others to accommodate. Kübler-Ross found that hospitals struggled with the anger expressed by those who were dying. In *On Grief and Grieving*, Kübler-Ross and Kessler suggest that our anger can isolate us from others just when we need them the most (Kübler-Ross 1969, p. 63; Kübler-Ross and Kessler 2005, p. 16). Christian communities may struggle particularly when that anger is directed at God. Kübler-Ross and Kessler tell the story of Heather, who felt enormous anger when her daughter died at 16. She was angry that her prayers had not been answered, and yet her anger was not seen as acceptable by her faith community. When warned about evoking the wrath of God, she replied: 'What is he going to do, take my daughter away? What's he going to do, take me? That would be fine. I'd rather be with her than be here.' At this point, it was suggested she pray for God's forgiveness. So she left the church and did not come back for years (Kübler-Ross and Kessler 2005, pp. 13–14). When we understand that anger is a natural and extremely common part of the grieving process, perhaps we will be more ready to accept angry grieving people in the Church, including people who are grieving their childlessness.

Depression is perhaps a little more acceptable, and yet still deeply uncomfortable for others to be around. Kübler-Ross and Kessler explain that depression protects grieving people by shutting down the nervous system while they start to adapt to a painful new reality. People may withdraw, stay at home all day crying, struggle to function. While the temptation may be to want grieving people to 'snap out of it', this is an important stage that needs to be fully experienced (Kübler-Ross and Kessler 2005, p. 21). It was at this stage in my grief that I realized I needed to take some time out. I was fortunate in being granted a three-month unpaid sabbatical from work, with some financial assistance towards the cost of counselling. I spent much of this three-month period deeply sad, sometimes tearful, spending a lot of time reading about infertility. Doubtless this reading would not have helped everyone, and there were times when I felt too sad and had to stop. And yet, the sadness was part of my healing. I had to feel it in order to be able to let it go.

Friends watching people grieving their childlessness say things to try to comfort them. *It's not the be-all and end-all. Children are hard work, you know – you're idealizing. You can do other things with your life; things that wouldn't be possible with kids. You can always adopt.* There is truth in all these statements, truth that perhaps becomes clearer with time. But they cannot take away the pain. People told me marriage was not the be-all and end-all before I got together with my husband, and yet there was an emptiness in my heart that went away when we found each other. I knew children were hard work, but the point was, I had not been given the option of having them. The idea that not having children would allow us to use our time differently just felt like a pressure to me – the pressure to make my life mean something because I would never be a mother. It also felt like a consolation prize. I knew we could explore adoption, but I had to grieve for my biological children before I could even consider that. And I knew that very few babies came up for adoption: we would very likely never hold our baby in our arms. That mattered. We would most likely miss out on the joys – as well as the pains – of infancy and early childhood. The pain of childlessness has to be felt, acknowledged, worked through and accepted before the childless person can accept any of the well-meaning, true – but in many ways unhelpful – consolations above. Kevin Ellis expresses the unending nature of childlessness well:

> The dance with childlessness will never really stop. It is true that there are other practical avenues that may legitimately be explored, from adoption to an inner resolve to give oneself to a particular cause or concern. Yet the music will go on as friends, colleagues and siblings become parents and then grandparents. Even those who tango with infertility assume that everyone else waltzes with potency. (Ellis 2003, p. 14)

When people have been able to feel and to work through their grief, they may reach the stage of acceptance. Kübler-Ross and Kessler explain that this is not the same as feeling all right about what has happened. Most people never feel all right about losing someone they love. People who want children and cannot have them are unlikely ever to feel that it is all right. But they can make their peace with their childlessness. After my sabbatical, when I had experienced much healing and started to look to the future with hope, I unexpectedly got into a long conversation about fertility with a stranger at my church's toddler group. 'I'm at peace with it,' I said, referring to the failure of IVF, and realized as I said it that it was true. 'I can see that,' said the 29-year-old mother of three children with whom I was talking. It would not be true to say that that was the end of my sadness. Various life events, not least the pressures of exploring adoption, have brought fresh waves of sadness that, at times, have bowled me over. And yet the hard work of grieving is, for the most part, behind me.

The consolation

When contemplating the painful experiences of life, we inevitably turn to the cross and resurrection of Christ. There is consolation to be found in this saving event: in the terrible crisis of the cross; in the dead pause on Holy Saturday, the body of Christ cold in the tomb; and in the glorious hope of Easter Sunday. Let us consider each in turn.

There are crises on the journey of childlessness: there are moments when the long-running ache becomes a sharp, stabbing pain. There are long-awaited appointments that may not go the way we had hoped, or that are cancelled at the last minute. There are diagnostic tests and fertility treatments that can be invasive, embarrassing, painful, emotionally demanding. There are test results that are not encouraging, which bring feelings of desperation and shame. There are negative pregnancy tests – so very many of them. When the pain reaches its peak, we turn to the agony of Christ on the cross and find a companion.

Serene Jones has written a gut-wrenchingly beautiful piece of theology in which she reflects on the experience of women suffering miscarriage and failed fertility treatment. In searching for a 'consoling image', she rests on the participation of the three persons of the Trinity in the event of the cross. Jones describes a woman whose fertility treatment fails, or whose pregnancies end in miscarriage, as carrying death within her body: the death of the embryo or foetus she longs so much to hold on to, but cannot. When Christ dies on the cross, Jones argues, death is taken up into the Godhead, and God carries death within Godself. A woman experiencing miscarriage or failed fertility treatment thus imitates the experience of the Trinity when the eternal Son submits to death in Jesus Christ. God too knows what it is to carry death within God's very self. This image cannot take away the pain; it may not even ease it. But it is an image into which a woman 'may crawl and curl up' (Jones 2009, pp. 129f.). It is an image that may help women and men of faith to recognize the powerful presence of the Almighty with them in their distinctive pain; a pain God has carried and, in a sense, still carries. God will always know what it is to carry death within Godself.

I have never experienced the trauma of miscarriage, and have the greatest of sympathy for all people who go through this agony. For a person who is struggling to conceive, how much more painful must the experience of miscarriage be. To experience the anxiety and pain of infertility; to achieve a pregnancy, only for that joyful event to end in heartbreak seems to me almost unbearably cruel. It is well known that miscarriage is common, for which reason the NHS does not generally investigate the cause until a woman has had three miscarriages. Jones has made an excellent start in exploring the distinctive pain of pregnancy loss. I would imagine that her work has the potential to offer deep consolation to women who have experienced the pain of miscarriage, engaging as it unflinchingly does with the brutal realities experienced by women whose insides are literally falling out. I suspect it is less helpful for men, however, and for women who, like me, have never been pregnant. My embryos never felt real to me because they never resulted in a positive pregnancy test. I have no way of knowing if any of them were even viable: many embryos are not capable of resulting in a pregnancy, and there is no way of knowing by looking at them.[4] We are in need of further consolation.

As I have already mentioned, childlessness is a cross that men bear as much as women. It is an un-sexing experience, whereby our gender identity is painfully undermined. Kevin Ellis has written powerfully about childlessness from a man's perspective. His comments on the theme of impotence highlight the association between virility and manliness. David Beckham, for example, has been nicknamed 'Goldenballs', both for his ability on the football pitch and his fathering of four children (Ellis 2003, p. 12). Some men can have issues with their sperm count or quality, or in rare cases no sperm at all – something over which they have no control, which is in no way the result of their actions. Likewise, a woman may discover that there are issues with the quality of her eggs, the lining of her uterus or the state of her fallopian tubes – again, something over which she has no control and that her actions have not caused. Her body has probably been shedding eggs every month since she was a teenager; she has gone through all the pain, embarrassment and inconvenience of menstruation month after month, year after year, and yet her body cannot do the one thing most women can do effortlessly. Childlessness makes men and women feel 'less than'; a man is supposed to be able to impregnate a woman; a woman is supposed to be able to conceive, and give birth to and care for children.

The experience creates shame in both sexes. It is also, for couples, a shared shame. In the case of infertility, one of the partners may be identified as 'responsible', with a particular impairment that makes it harder for their body to do its part in conception. This can be a bitter pill to swallow. In roughly one-third of cases where the cause of the infertility has been identified, the man is sub-fertile; in another third, the woman has some kind of fertility impairment; in the remainder of cases there is an issue with both partners. In a significant number of cases, there is no identifiable cause (Winston 2015, chapter 2). Regardless of the cause, however, where a couple are struggling to conceive it is a shared grief and a shared shame, because this is something for which they need each other, and which together they cannot do. Even when there is no clinically diagnosed 'fault' with a male partner, he may be frustrated with his impotence in the situation – unable to get his partner pregnant, unable to take away her pain or dry her tears. Even when the woman has no diagnosed impairment, she may feel less feminine, a failure as a woman in some way, because she has not been able to become a mother. In a small number of cases, earlier lifestyle choices may possibly be a factor – for example, if either partner has contracted chlamydia, a sexually transmitted disease that can be symptomless and yet cause infertility. Even where this is the case, however, there obviously would have been no intention of bringing about infertility. Individuals and couples can castigate themselves for waiting too long to start a family – and if *they* do not, society certainly will. It has become axiomatic that women today 'put their careers first', not paying attention to the ticking fertility timebomb.[5] Many people have no choice when it comes to starting a family, however, with people meeting their life partner and settling down later in life than their parents and grandparents did.

Regardless of the medical reason for the infertility, if there is one, diagnosis and treatment are demeaning for both sexes. A woman becomes used to lying semi-naked on a couch, legs apart, while medical professionals explore her sex organs with a variety of metal and plastic implements. A man becomes used to sitting in a room with a small plastic cup, perhaps with a pile of pornographic magazines, while medical staff wait for him to make his contribution to the process. The 2018 Netflix film *Private Life* brilliantly portrays the mortifications of fertility treatment for both sexes. The husband, played by Paul Giamatti, is shown sitting in a room in the clinic with his trousers down, trying to change the channel on the TV from which a porn film is loudly playing. There is nothing sexy about it at all. The wife, played by Kathryn Hahn, is shown lying back on a couch in a hospital gown while a doctor holding a speculum asks her if she likes prog rock. The couple are in their forties, and after a failed treatment it is suggested that they consider egg donation to give themselves a better chance of conceiving. Their niece, who is in her twenties, wants to help them start a family and agrees to donate some of her eggs. In a scene that echoed some of my own experiences, she is shown coming out of an appointment in tears, saying that the doctor 'yelled at her' because her ovaries are not responding well to hormone stimulation. She does not have enough follicles growing quickly enough. He would expect a woman of her age to be producing much more much faster.[6] Thus the shame of the couple's infertility affects their niece too, shamed for not responding well enough to the treatment. Even among those individuals and couples unfortunate enough to need IVF, there is a wide variety of experience. To know already that your body is not doing what it should, and then to discover that it is not responding to the one treatment that has the promise of helping you, is mortifying indeed.

In this very personal, very private shame, which goes to the root of what it means to be a woman, to be a man, let us consider Christa. In 1975 the artist Edwina Sandys first exhibited *Christa*, a sculpture of a naked female Christ on the cross.[7] Sculpted in clay and cast in bronze, Christa is gaunt, sad, beautiful, and obviously female. She has broad hips and full breasts, one knee bent, which emphasizes the womanliness of her painfully thin body. The crown of thorns rests on her long hair. The image of a female Christ on the cross is intriguing, perhaps disturbing, potentially healing. Christa draws our attention to overlooked aspects of the gospel narrative. The soldiers' mocking of Jesus before his crucifixion is well known, but the sexual humiliation to which he is subjected is something not often touched upon by preachers. Serene Jones goes so far as to refer to Jesus as a 'victim of sexual abuse', pointing to the fact that he is stripped by the soldiers who mock him, putting him into a scarlet robe and crowning him with a crown of thorns, before stripping him once again and putting his own clothes on him.[8] We are used to images of Christ on the cross that modestly cover his nakedness with a loincloth. This does not represent the reality of first-century Roman executions, and Christa's naked, tortured, female body reminds us of this. A man subject to the mortification of ejaculating into a plastic cup may resonate with Christ's sexual humiliation as he hung naked on the cross. A woman who is pierced by a speculum, an ultrasound probe, an endless succession of needles, finds a companion in Christ nailed to the cross.

In contemplation of Christa, women and men experiencing infertility may find a companion in their shame. Christ was naked and vulnerable, his male body revealed to a mocking world. He too was powerless to change his situation. We may understand Christ to have chosen to stay powerless despite the fact he could have saved himself. Alternatively, we may understand the self-emptying of the eternal Son in the incarnation to have stripped Christ of his divine power. Whether we see Christ experiencing powerlessness or choosing it, in contemplating his cross we see someone who understands what it is to be naked and vulnerable, your body exposed to the world.

And then he dies. After the cross, for two nights and a day – nothing. If the much-desired baby does not come along, there comes a point when the realization starts to sink in that the journey of childlessness has come to an unsatisfactory ending. There is so much that can be done to help people experiencing infertility and childlessness: diagnostic tests, drug treatments, surgery, ultimately IVF. And yet, two-thirds of people will go through the trauma of IVF and still not have a baby to show for it.[9] Eventually, some people will find that their childlessness is likely to be permanent, and then, after the cross of fertility investigations and treatments, they find themselves in the tomb with Christ, all hope gone. The tomb on Holy Saturday was a place of silence, stillness, death, sterility. All hope had perished. There was nothing more to hope for. Usually we rush to the resurrection, knowing the end of the story. But for people who find their childlessness to be a permanent condition, resurrection seems to be out of reach. They are, in a sense, living in Holy Saturday. Their Holy Saturday drags on and on, with no end in sight. Perhaps one day new life will come with the joy of a pregnancy; perhaps they will adopt a child who will bring new life to their family; perhaps they will grieve, move on and find they are able to give birth to other things. But for the time being, there they are in the tomb. Here, life comes to an end for the incarnate Christ; here he shares my barrenness: 'It is here in death that the incarnate god is incapable, impotent, barren and infertile' (Ellis 2003, p. 13).

As a woman who has never been able to achieve a pregnancy, and who has come to the realization that she never will, I find myself identifying less now with the cross than with the grave of Holy Saturday. In the grave, Christ becomes my companion in hopelessness. Christ 'joins [me] in the solitude of death and judgement, so that [I am] solitary no longer, and do not have to die alone' (Lewis 2001, p. 439). Christ becomes barren, like me, and I become a little bit like Christ:

> ... the dead body of Jesus wrapped in the tomb with all hope of life seemingly at an end sanctifies my childlessness. Not only does it sanctify, for me, it actually blesses my childless state, which as a person of faith, gives me strength to continue on. (Ellis 2006, p. 25)

The day after the crucifixion makes me think of the time after a funeral, when the crisis of the illness or accident is past, the official acknowledgement of the death has taken place, and then all but those closest to the person who has died move on with their lives. Then the grieving are left to the forever task of living with what has been lost. Childlessness has its crises, its moments of hope, the dashing of that hope, and then the rest of a lifetime without the hoped-for child. Just like other griefs, there is the dull business of life always being a bit worse, for ever. Part of the cruelty of childlessness is that there is almost always hope. A single childless person may meet a partner soon with whom they might have a child. A childless person in a relationship may achieve a 'miracle baby'. It is almost never possible for doctors to say a person is sterile, utterly incapable of creating new life. In equally rare cases a man may have no sperm at all in his semen (a condition called azoospermia); in rare cases a woman may have had an early menopause or a hysterectomy. And yet, for those with the money or the access to credit, there is egg donation, sperm donation, surrogacy. There are so many ways to make the dream happen. And so there has to come a point where a person, or a couple, say 'no more'. There has to be a line drawn. There has to be the death of a hope so that there can be mourning – the painful business of learning to live with loss. People often say to the childless, 'there is always adoption'. Yes, there is, but adoption agencies very wisely refuse to consider individuals and couples who have not yet given up on the miracle promised by medical science. Generally, they insist on a break of at least six months between finishing fertility treatment and beginning the adoption process. They need to be reassured that prospective adopters have given up hope and grieved their loss before they can start on the long road of becoming adoptive parents.

Between the cross and the possibility of resurrection, there is a pause. Holy Saturday is not often celebrated in churches and has not often been considered by theologians. It is an in-between day. It is the pause between cross and resurrection; between death and life; between despair and hope. Nothing happens on Holy Saturday. The crisis is over, life has come to an end. The Bible tells us almost nothing about this day. The only Gospel writer who tells us anything about the time between Christ's death and resurrection is Matthew, who recounts the sealing of Christ's tomb to prevent his body being stolen (Matt. 27.62–66). A. E. Lewis, one of a small number of theologians in modern times to consider Holy Saturday,[10] points out that we who live on the other side of the resurrection see Holy Saturday from our point of view. We see it as the pause before something wonderful happens. And yet, for the people living at the time, it was a dead end. They did not know that it was not the end of the story (Lewis 2001, pp. 29–31). Christ had died, and nothing was more permanent than death. He had saved others, but he had not been able to save himself. The first Holy Saturday was an ending, and we need endings.

In that tomb, the Son of God identifies with a human corpse (Lewis 2001, p. 27). God, the eternal God, submits Godself to human limitation. The One who is all-powerful, ever-present, comes to a dead end in one place in time and space. In that dead end, God identifies with all those of us who have reached our own dead ends. Those of us who cannot create new life carry barrenness within our bodies. In the lifeless body of Christ, the triune God identifies with our lifelessness. The One whose creative love makes all things possible experiences the ultimate human limitation of death.

Childlessness can be bitter and it can be ugly. The desire to give birth to new life; to share one's home with children; to watch them grow and care for them with tenderness: these are all good impulses that, when thwarted, start to rot. To refuse to rejoice in another's happy news; to look on someone else's beautiful children with anger and resentment; to view another's swollen belly with outrage: these are not attractive emotions. They are deeply uncomfortable. And yet they must be felt and acknowledged. They need not be expressed openly and in public, but they must be expressed. Repressing them does not make them go away. Elaine Tyler May's respondents eloquently expressed their bitterness and anger in the letters they wrote her. Lydia explained:

> The world turns and we stand still ... I detest all pregnant women – whether they are my friends or not. They carry their pregnancy like a badge of honor, when they did nothing special to achieve it. Honestly, they make me sick. Sounds pretty bad, doesn't it? I'm becoming more cynical about it as I get older and my clock ticks away.

Seeing others' pregnant bellies, others' children, made them feel 'hateful – even murderous'. One woman confessed she had fantasized about running over a family with small children in her car, because she saw them enjoying a joyful family life which had so far eluded her (Tyler May 1995, p. 225).

Christ's beautiful living human body was given over to death and decay; it began to decompose in that tomb. For this reason, perhaps our bitter, ugly emotions – the natural desire to bring forth life, thwarted and killed and now rotting inside us – perhaps even these emotions can be enveloped, embraced and held within the love of God. Those friends who helped me the most when I was at my most bitter and unhappy showed me grace by never telling me everything was all right. They never tried to make me feel better. By allowing my pain to be, they allowed me my Holy Saturday: my time of hopelessness.

Sieger Köder's painting *Holy Saturday* shows the dead Christ lying, wrapped in a sheet, with the red light of dawn just beginning to show through the gap between the stone and the doorway. Properly, this is not Holy Saturday any more, but is the moment of resurrection. Miraculously, graciously, after death comes life once more. Jesus was dead, but now he is alive. People struggling with childlessness begin by imagining that resurrection will come with the longed-for baby. I doubt anyone starts fertility treatment believing that they will be among the two-thirds who are unsuccessful. I entered my first cycle of IVF believing each cycle had a 40 per cent chance of working. I was wrong. Calculating the probability of success is far more complex than that and, after several failed embryo transfers, the odds of success go down. I did not know this at the time. I did not really believe we would finish two cycles having got nowhere. Not even contemplating a third cycle because the first two had failed so miserably. I believed – really believed – that resurrection would come for us in the person of a baby. After all, everyone has a miracle story. Everyone, I imagine, believes at some point that a miracle will be granted them. Even if the miracle never happens, however, resurrection is possible. Indeed, resurrection is assured.

What is the hope of resurrection to a person struggling with childlessness? To some it is the hope that one day they will meet the babies they have lost. And who knows but that, in God's mercy, they may? But resurrection is not just for the future. Resurrection is a present reality as well as a future hope. Resurrection comes at the end of the journey of grief, when people start to invest themselves in new relationships, new possibilities. A friend of mine gave me a beautiful analogy: it was given at a time when I still had high hopes of conceiving, but I remembered it after all hope was lost. It is the image of a garden where there has been a large and beautiful tree that has died and been removed. It leaves a gaping hole; but its death allows other things to grow.[11] We know we are in the season of resurrection when other things start to grow. For my husband and me, one of the things that began to grow was our desire to adopt. This is not a choice every childless person would wish to make. Becoming an adoptive parent – parenting a traumatized child – this is one of the plants that may grow in the garden of resurrection.

Once baby fever has subsided, every pregnant woman you see stops being a reminder of what has been denied and instead becomes a sign of a parallel life, one that has diverged from yours: not better, just different. While I was still in my Holy Saturday, I used to loathe fighting my way through the pre-school parents queueing up to drop off their children at the church where I worked. They were a daily reminder of what I was not, of what I did not have. Once I had been raised from my grief, I could look on someone else's child and smile.

Resurrection can come with the realization – as one of Madelyn Cain's interviewees so beautifully expressed it – that we give birth to many things (Cain 2001, p. 148). Human creativity and possibility have not stopped just because our flesh has not brought forth new flesh. Grief itself can be powerfully creative (this book was conceived in the midst of my grief). It is too simple, and in some ways crass, to say that there are possibilities open to a childless person or couple that are not open to their friends who are parents. World travel, for example; clutter-free homes; disposable income. These are pleasant things, but not really much of a consolation when compared with what has been lost. More profound than that, however: human creativity and possibility can still flourish when one hope has died. There are other things to hope for. There are other children than our flesh-babies. This is explored further in Chapter 4.

'Christ is Risen' by Matt Maher and Mia Fieldes was a song I listened to again and again while I awaited resurrection.[12] I found myself enchanted by the beauty of the resurrection even as I waited to be raised myself. And the resurrection of Christ seemed to be summoning me to action. The Greek verbs *anhistemi* and *egeiro*, both used in relation to the resurrection, can be translated 'awaken' or 'rouse' (Brown 1978, pp. 259, 279). Through the song, God seemed to be gently and lovingly beckoning me to rouse myself from the slumber of my sorrow and to begin to live in resurrection. Perhaps resurrection comes as we wake up to new possibilities, rousing ourselves from the much-needed slumber of grief to start living once again.

Resurrection does not reverse or eliminate the pain, however. The risen Christ still bears the marks on his hands and feet and the wound in his side. Kevin Ellis is an adoptive parent who describes himself as, in a sense, a 'childless father'. He and his wife were unable to conceive because of his infertility. Despite being the proud father of a son he adores, childlessness is still part of his identity. The pain of being unable to father a biological child remains alongside his deep love for his son (Ellis 2013, pp. 130–1).

I wonder whether there is an element of defiance in resurrection. Choosing to stand up and to carry on in the face of great loss. *Anhistemi* also carries the connotation of a political uprising (Brown 1978, p. 259). Perhaps resurrection could be an act of protest against the cruelty of loss. Perhaps, in this life, we experience resurrection when we go through terrible experiences and find, eventually, that we are able to get up again and go on living. Harold Kushner, whose son died from a rare genetic condition at the age of 14, resists all attempts to rationalize or to soften life's most painful experiences: 'We do not try to explain it. We do not justify it ... We do not even accept it. We survive it. We recognize its unfairness and defiantly choose to go on living'.[13]

Writers on grief insist that loss is not something people 'get over', but that they learn to live with, and that eventually stops consuming them. Megan Devine has spoken powerfully of the tragic sudden death of her partner some years ago. She has experienced much healing, but she is not 'back to normal', and never will be. In her book, *It's OK That You're Not OK: Meeting Grief and Loss in a Culture That Doesn't Understand*, she writes of 'the wild howl at the center of grief'. She insists that there is a deep pain which the passage of time does not erase: 'Sometimes I say there's a screaming there that has never stopped, and probably never will. What I've found in the now almost eight years since that happened is that I found a way to live with the screaming.'[14]

The scars on the body of the risen Christ remind us that the Christ on the cross of Good Friday is the same Christ who was raised. Cross and resurrection are for ever connected (Craddock 1990, p. 290). When we consider the grieving childless person in the light of cross and resurrection, we are able to affirm both the terrible loss they have suffered and the hope of Easter Sunday. Resurrection is sometimes incorrectly seen as an affirmation of the immortality of the soul – that there is something in us that death cannot destroy. This view owes more to Greek philosophy than biblical revelation. The biblical writers did not see body and soul as separate entities, but as a whole that was wholly destroyed in death. A biblical understanding of the resurrection is that Christ really died, body and soul, and that God raised him from death (Brown 1978, pp. 286–304).

For people coming to terms with childlessness, as for all those who grieve, this knowledge has tremendous power. Because Christ really died, we do not have to tell childless people that what they have lost does not really matter. We do not have to attempt to cheer them up with banalities about disposable income and holidays. We can accept that, for them, hope has been obliterated. And because Christ was raised from death, we can hold out the hope that their terrible loss can and will be raised too. Resurrection may come partly in the acceptance that they may reach once they have fully grieved their loss. Resurrection may come as new things grow in the garden of resurrection – new possibilities, projects, interests and plans. Ultimately, I suspect grieving people will experience resurrection in all its fullness only when Christ comes again and death is swallowed up in victory (1 Cor. 15.54). If God can raise my material body from death, decay, cremation; if God can raise my personality, my idiosyncrasies, my talents and weaknesses; if God can raise everything that I am from the dead, because God wants to, because God is love: then God can and will raise my broken hopes and dreams. God can and will raise my childlessness.

The practice

The day we were told there was 'no clinical reason to continue' with fertility treatment was a Monday. The following Sunday I led a service at my church on the theme of lament. It was August, and we had planned a series of stand-alone Sunday morning services on various psalms. When planning the series several weeks earlier, my colleague and I had agreed to choose a variety of psalms representing different moods – praise, wisdom, confession and lament. I had volunteered to preach on lament, and chose Psalm 6:

> I am weary with my moaning;
> every night I flood my bed with tears;
> I drench my couch with my weeping.
> My eyes waste away because of grief;
> they grow weak because of all my foes. (Ps. 6.6–7)

I did not know when I chose that theme that I would be reeling from the total failure of our fertility treatment when I preached it. Living through months and years of waiting, hoping, testing, treatment and repeated disappointment, however, had caused me to be more and more drawn to themes of sadness and brokenness. There are more psalms of lament than of any other kind. Many scholars believe that the psalms were used liturgically in Jewish temple worship: lament was part of the worship of the people of Israel (see, for example, Barton and Bowden 2004, p. 31). Christian worship in our day – certainly in Western Europe and North America – contains very little, if any, lament. I felt intuitively that there was discomfort with lament: certainly, in the Baptist churches and Christian conferences that had provided my chief experiences of worship. I decided to explore why this was. My sermon title was a question: 'What's the problem with lament?' Several reasons occurred to me. First, it hurts, and we don't like to be hurt. Second, it makes us feel powerless, and this is frightening (we will consider the theme of powerlessness further in Chapter 3). Third, we may worry that we dishonour God with our lament.

Our bodies instinctively flinch away from any source of pain, and our minds do the same. Perhaps it is only in counselling and other psychological therapies that we intentionally allow ourselves to really feel and to sit with our pain, in the hope that we might understand its source and thus ease it. The awkwardness we feel around people who are grieving, considered in Chapter 1, perhaps arises partly from the fact that we know they are hurting, which reminds us of our own capacity to hurt; it reminds us of our own mortality and of the mortality of those around us. This is not only painful but frightening, because it is something over which we have so little control. Grieving people are people in pain, and we do not like pain, or the helplessness we feel in the face of it. Jody Day is a trained psychotherapist, and explains the effect that other people's pain has on us: 'Whether we realise it consciously or not, we humans, to a greater or lesser degree, feel each other's emotions – the mirror neurons in our brain fire when we see someone experiencing an emotion so that we feel the same' (Day 2016, p. 86). When we spend time with someone in pain, we literally hurt along with them. And so the automatic response, much of the time, is to try to make their pain go away so that ours will too: '… when others tell us about a miracle baby story, what they may be doing is using those stories as an unconscious shield to stop us feeling our pain so they can stop feeling what it triggers in them – their ungrieved losses' (Day, pp. 86–7). Day writes much about 'grief work', arguing that it is possible to integrate our losses, to recover and to experience hope, if we allow ourselves to grieve properly. 'Ungrieved losses' are presumably those losses that have remained unacknowledged, unfelt and hence unresolved. Christians who meet the sadness of childless people with stories of miracles, exhortations to pray harder or insistence that it is 'all part of God's plan' may be driven more by avoidance of their own pain than by piety.

Some streams of Christian spirituality seem to promote the view that true faith meets every grief and disappointment with calm acceptance and simple trust. This leaves little room for lament, which may be seen to demonstrate a lack of faith in the goodness of God. Sustained reflection on the cross and tomb of Christ must surely offer excellent grounds for faithful lament, however. Christ did not leap straight from the cross to the resurrection in the blink of an eye. He truly suffered, he truly died and, for a time, he stayed truly dead. Christ shared our suffering, our isolation and even our death, and thus sadness, grief and hopelessness are taken up into the Godhead. We worship a Messiah who was afraid of death and who suffered as he died. Thus, every area of our lives, including the most difficult and painful, are held in the love and grace and mercy of God, and our worship must help our people understand that. Our worship must include lament. We have to find ways of expressing sadness, brokenness, grief and desolation in public worship.

The service I led based on Psalm 6 was a short child-friendly service, during which a clip was shown from the wonderful Pixar film *Inside Out*. The film tells the story of a happy-go-lucky 11-year-old girl called Riley who is struggling to cope with her family's house move and her separation from all her friends and everything she has known and loved. The story is told mostly from the perspective of the five emotions inside her head: Joy, Sadness, Anger, Fear and Disgust. Riley has until now been a very happy girl, and thus Joy is very much in charge inside her head. Unfortunately, the new family circumstances mean that Sadness keeps interfering and casting everything with a gloomy blue glow. During the course of the film, Joy learns that Sadness has an important role to play and, finally, she learns to let Sadness do her job. In one very clever scene in the film, Joy is trying to cheer up Bing-Bong, Riley's imaginary friend from early childhood. As Riley has grown older, she has forgotten Bing-Bong, and he is crying. Joy is impatient to get going on her journey, and is trying to chivvy Bing-Bong along. This is not working. Then Sadness goes and sits next to him. She listens to his woes and agrees that his situation is very sad. Bing-Bong cries for a while, then dries his tears, gets up and carries on with the journey. Joy is astonished that Sadness has managed to do what she cannot. This is the power of Sadness; the power of lament. Sometimes we just need to cry. And that emotional release enables us to keep going.

It may not have been wise to have carried on and led this service mere days after such a crushing disappointment. The wisest thing for most people would probably have been to have claimed some compassionate leave and left the service to others. I think, for me, it was a way of expressing my grief, however. I did not have the freedom to share my sadness with the congregation at that time. So I did what I was able to do: I preached a sermon that expressed how I was feeling, and exhorted the congregation to accept the lament that, privately, I knew I needed to express myself.

Almost exactly a year after this service, I attended a Christian conference with a group from my church and discovered a spirituality that seemed to have almost entirely edited out pain. Jesus was worshipped as triumphant risen Lord, mighty in battle, powerfully at work in the world through the prayers of his people. Much time was given to prayers for healing. Testimonies of healing and of triumphing over adversity were repeatedly told. My pain was no longer raw and I had experienced much emotional healing by this point, but still I spent most of the week in a state of repressed fury. As the others in my group were having a great time and I did not want to ruin their fun, I kept my thoughts mostly to myself. Instead, I wrote a short parable in my journal, which I have reproduced below. I was inspired by the work of Pete Rollins, author of *The Orthodox Heretic.*[15] Rollins tells stories that cleverly and deliberately subvert our expectations to make us reflect on our views of Christ and of the Christian life. I wondered what a conference that was shaped by Christ crucified, suffering for his suffering world, might look like:

The festival was held every year. Christians gathered from all over the country, in church or social groups, to spend a few days together worshipping God. They loved being together; they loved the energy that was generated by so many worshippers gathered together with one purpose.

In the mornings they attended Bible studies taught by world-renowned scholars. People got up early and queued up with their Bibles, notebooks and early morning coffee to hear the great teachers. They listened as gradually their biblical knowledge was stripped away little by little, and they left every session knowing less than they had when they went in.

In the afternoons, many people attended a great marketplace in the middle of the venue where tables were piled high with books, clothing and other supplies. People brought bags of good-quality clothes to be donated to homeless charities; Bibles to be sent to countries where most Christians could not afford or even get hold of a Bible; toys and other trinkets to be sold in charity shops to raise money for good causes. Day by day the piles increased, and volunteers sifted through the mountains of stuff, sorting donations.

It was in the evenings that the really exciting things happened, however. Thousands gathered in the largest of the venues as the worship band began to play beautiful songs of lament. Everyone cried as they wept for love of God's hurting world. Then someone got up to speak about the power of prayer. People with a special story to tell were invited to step forward. They spoke of chronic illnesses; devastating bereavements; painful failures. Then a time of prayer ministry began. The happy and the whole came forward and people laid hands on them and prayed. The Spirit moved in great power, and they walked away limping.[16]

Notes

1 Dave Lowrie writes movingly of the agony his wife has gone through repeatedly through six miscarriages: Dave Lowrie, 2018, 'She's Incredible Too. #BabyLossAwarenessWeek', *Saltwater and Honey*, 15 October, http://saltwaterandhoney.org/blog/shes-incredible-too-baby-loss-awareness-week, accessed 1.11.2018.

2 The difference between embryos lost in fertility treatment and other miscarriages is the probability of failure. Most pregnancies detected in the usual way do not end in miscarriage, whereas most IVF embryos are lost. This is also true of 'natural' conception – most embryos do not implant, and yet the woman is unlikely to realize she has conceived before the embryo is lost.

3 Kübler-Ross and Kessler do not refer specifically to childlessness, but explain the different ways in which bargaining shows itself.

4 Robert Winston suggests that on average only about 18 per cent of normal-looking embryos would produce a viable pregnancy and birth. See Winston 2015, chapter 7.

5 For example, see: Mark Tran, 2014, 'Kirstie Allsopp tells young women: ditch university and have a baby by 27', *The Guardian*, 2 June, www.theguardian.com/tv-and-radio/2014/jun/02/kirstie-allsop-young-women-ditch-university-baby-by-27, accessed 1.11.2018.

6 A woman's body typically produces one follicle containing one egg per menstrual cycle. IVF involves stimulating the ovaries to produce lots of follicles in the hope that lots of eggs – ideally 10–14 – can be collected. The development of the follicles is regularly measured in the days leading up to egg collection.

7 www.edwinasandys.com/about, accessed 1.11.2018.

8 @SereneJones, https://twitter.com/SereneJones/status/104749994 6923057152, accessed 3.10.2018.

9 '2018 trends in fertility treatment', *Human Fertilisation & Embryology Authority*, www.hfea.gov.uk/about-us/news-and-press-re leases/2020-news-and-press-releases/2018-trends-in-fertility-treatment/, accessed 1.8.2020.

10 I am only aware of A. E. Lewis, Hans Urs von Balthasar and Shelly Rambo.

11 Inspired by Sittser 2004, p. 51.

12 © 2009 Be Essential Songs (admin. by Essential Music Publish-

ing LLC); Upside Down Under (admin. by Essential Music Publishing LLC); spiritandsong.com (admin. by Integrity Music); Thankyou Music (admin. by Integrity Music).

13 Kushner, introduction to 20th anniversary edition of *When Bad Things Happen to Good People*.

14 Transcript of interview with Megan Devine, www.resources. soundstrue.com/transcript/megan-devine-the-howl-at-the-center-of-grief/, accessed 17.1.2021.

15 Rollins 2009.

16 This short reflection was first published in 2020, *Gathering Up the Crumbs: Celebrating a Century of Accredited, Ordained, Baptist Women in Ministry in the UK*, Catriona Gorton et al. (eds) Didcot: Baptist Union of Great Britain.

3

Powerless

I am completely helpless in the face of whatever it is nature appears to be doing here ... I cannot change these things, even though I desire to do so more than anything else I have ever desired. (Jones 2009, pp. 134–5)

The experience

More often than not, fertility treatment fails. There is so much that can be done to help people experiencing infertility; everyone knows someone who has been successful in assisted reproduction. But there are far more people who are ultimately disappointed.[1] In 2018, IVF patients under 35 had a birth rate of 31 per cent per embryo transferred (23 per cent for all patients).[2] Suzi Leather, former chair of the Human Fertilisation and Embryology Authority, acknowledges the pain behind these statistics: 'Three quarters [of patients] are going through all that distress, expense, discomfort and waiting and at the end of it, they are not pregnant' (Ellis 2006, p. 5). Those whose infertility takes the form of recurrent miscarriage – who are able to conceive, but not able to carry a baby to term – are in an equally painful position. Very often it is not even possible to determine why a woman keeps miscarrying, let alone to do anything to help her.[3] Ultimately, no one but God has the power to create life. Those of us who remain childless have to come to terms with that immovable fact.

At times, the frustration of wanting something so badly that did not happen made me feel almost as if I were going mad. On the one hand, there was advice – both medical and pseudo-medical – about maximizing our chances. What to eat, what (not) to drink, which vitamins to take, which holistic therapies might help, how often to have sex. At the same time, from various sources, variations on the theme, 'just relax and it will happen'. Should I relax and let it happen, I wondered, or should I be working hard to ensure that it did? Ultimately, our fertility treatment failed, and we had to begin the process of coming to terms with our infertility.

Many of us in the affluent global north are used to having a high degree of control over our lives. If we want something, we get it, or work towards it, or save for it. This is, of course, a peculiarly middle-class privilege which not all enjoy, even in relatively wealthy countries. Those of us with enough education and self-confidence to get a job, with enough money to pay our bills, and without a disability, are used to a high degree of personal agency. When those of us who are used to getting what we want in life experience unwanted childlessness, at first we carry this attitude into our fertility struggle. We buy and read books with tips and advice. We lose weight, give up smoking, cut down our alcohol consumption. Straight women who are in a relationship follow their cycle and choose to have sex at their most fertile times. Women and men go to the GP and ask for fertility tests, and ultimately can be referred for fertility treatments such as IUI and IVF. It may be at this point that some of us start to realize the limits of our power. Some people find that their area's clinical commissioning group (CCG) will authorize three rounds of IVF through the NHS: they are the lucky ones. Most people will find, however, that their CCG will only authorize two cycles, or just one, or maybe none at all.[4] Others may discover that, even though their CCG will authorize treatment, they don't meet the criteria. Perhaps the woman is over 40 – in which case, she is likely to have to pay for her own treatment. Perhaps one partner has children from a previous relationship, in which case any treatment may have to be self-funded. Of course, even here, inequality persists. Some individuals or couples may well be able to afford to fund treatment themselves, may be able to access credit, or may be able to borrow from family to pay for IUI or IVF. For many, this will not be an option.

Patience was a virtue in very short supply when I was considering fertility treatment. By the time we realized that we were having trouble conceiving, I was 35. By the time we had had all the necessary tests, waited for all the consultants' appointments to come through, and been referred for IVF, I was 37. I lost count of the number of times I was told to be patient, while knowing that my fertility was declining with every passing year. And yet, because most women can conceive naturally even in their late thirties, given time, medical professionals are in no hurry to push through the necessary tests. Rosemary Morgan points out that these delays are, in part, a diagnostic tool: infertility can only be determined after a certain amount of time without a pregnancy (Morgan 2013, p. 9). It is only natural to worry, once several months have gone by without a positive pregnancy test, but doctors will not generally feel it necessary to perform any diagnostic tests until a year has gone by, unless the female partner is in her late thirties or forties, in which case it may be possible to get tested sooner.[5]

Then a GP referral for tests is needed. Depending on the results of those tests, there may be a referral to the fertility clinic. These appointments take a long time to come through, and several appointments will generally be needed before a referral for IVF. We came back a day early from holiday once for a hospital appointment, only to find an answerphone message cancelling the appointment and rebooking it for seven weeks later. Even once a person has been referred for IVF, they may find themselves on a waiting list, depending on the demand in their area. None of this makes for patience. Patience is a tall order. And yet, it is very difficult to make good decisions when we are in a hurry. The feeling that the clock is ticking and *someone needs to do something or it will be too late* ... this does not make for calm reflection when considering choices in treatment. I hated becoming a stereotype: the hysterical infertile woman in her thirties. Looking back, I can see how unkind this stereotype is, and I judge myself less harshly. The anxiety is only natural, in a situation with such high stakes, where you are so powerless, with a ticking biological clock, and at the mercy of an overstretched NHS which does not move quickly. There is nothing about the situation that makes for calm or for patience.

There comes a point, sooner or later, when – if they do not have a baby – people struggling with childlessness will come to the end of their power. This is sooner if they're older, or poorer, or unlucky enough to be less fertile or less responsive to treatment. Later, if they're younger or wealthier. But many do come to the end of their ability to create the life for which they had hoped, a life that they see others achieving easily. This is a bitter realization. Dr Richard Marrs, an American fertility expert, sees this time and again in women undergoing treatment: '[Most of the women I see are] flabbergasted because they could achieve everything else they set out for and they're stunned they can't do this' (Cain 2001, p. 60). Practical theologian Heather Walton was in exactly this position. She writes: 'I am sussed, streetwise and I am clever. I haven't failed in anything I have tried since I was 10 years old. No, that's not true. I fail driving tests and I fail pregnancy tests. For five years I've been failing pregnancy tests' (Walton 2003, p. 201).

This sense of frustration and failure does not only affect women. Infertility specialist Dr Mark Trolice experienced a decade of infertility before he and his wife adopted their children. He has not only seen this powerlessness in the people he has treated, but has experienced it for himself: 'I always feel responsible for my family, to do everything I can to make everything go perfect, and make things better, and I couldn't help my wife … I just couldn't believe there was nothing I could do to help her.'[6]

For Heather Walton, her infertility was almost the only area of her life where she could not achieve success. Her image of herself as talented and capable was shattered by her inability to achieve a pregnancy. For Mark Trolice, his self-image as protector, provider and fixer was badly damaged. He was unable to protect his wife from the pain of their infertility; unable to provide a baby; unable to fix this situation. People struggling with childlessness can experience terrible blows to their self-esteem: their image of themselves as capable – and perhaps successful – people is painfully undermined due to their incapability, their failure.

In a bleak and beautiful chapter that explores miscarriage

and failed fertility treatment, Serene Jones acknowledges the 'radical loss of agency' faced by people who go through these experiences (Jones 2009, pp. 134–5). The words of her friend Wendy are quoted at the beginning of this chapter. Wendy is 'completely helpless' in the face of her body's inability to hold on to the child she has conceived. As a person of faith, that utter powerlessness is experienced before a God who, we are so often told, is omnipotent. A God whose hands made the stars; who sees the sparrow fall and counts the hairs on our heads; whose eyes saw our unformed bodies and knit us together in our mothers' wombs (Gen. 1.16; Matt. 10.29–30; Ps. 139.13–16). A God who created everything and who loves every part of creation deeply and individually, and yet has not granted us our heart's desire. A God who, the Bible tells us, gives to those who ask persistently in faith (Luke 11.5–10). While trying to come to terms with the ultimate frustration of my hopes, I looked around for reading material to help me. Many of the books written from a Christian perspective seemed to me to peddle variations on the theme 'God sees the bigger picture'. I found myself becoming angry. It seemed that they were all busy defending God and not really listening to the pain – perhaps not their own, and certainly not mine. Well-meaning people of faith often say, or write, that everything that happens is part of God's plan: God is in control, even if we do not understand or cannot perceive the reasons for our suffering. This kind of response seems to me to fail to engage with the depth of sorrow of those who suffer deeply, including those of us who are involuntarily childless. This kind of response denies our feelings by shutting down the conversation. It dismisses questions and doubts by asserting that the universe is orderly and that all is well, even if we do not like it.

Trusting God is an important theme in Christian spirituality, and having faith a non-negotiable mark of piety. What does it mean to 'trust God' or to 'have faith' when God is letting you down so badly and common sense tells you that there is no guarantee of a happy ending? All the well-meaning pieties sounded very hollow in my ears. I saw people all around me who had achieved easily what I could not, or who had struggled against the odds and eventually, perhaps miraculously, been granted children. But there was no miracle for me. The theological question became very simple and very stark: did God lack the power to grant my wish, or had God chosen not to? It is the question so many millions of people have asked themselves over the centuries, often suffering losses far greater than my own.

In his substantial study of Holy Saturday, A. E. Lewis writes about human limitation. He argues that we human beings have to come to terms with our limits. The ultimate human limit is, of course, our mortality (Lewis 2001, pp. 411f.). A woman has to come to terms with the limits of her fertility. There is not all the time in the world. At some point in her late twenties or early thirties every woman, if she wants children and is not yet a mother, starts thinking about how many fertile years she has left. What is less well known is that male fertility also declines with age, albeit less steeply than women's. American fertility doctor Mark Trolice estimates that a man in his early forties is half as fertile as a man under 25, is likely to take five times as long to conceive, and his partner will have an increased risk of miscarriage.[7] Hysterical headlines scream about the ticking clock, and yet many of us have very little control over when we can have children. I would not have chosen to wait until I was 30 to find my life partner. I didn't know that I would not be in the 80 per cent of women who conceive with relative ease in their mid- and late thirties.[8] There is so much we do not know and cannot control, and a painful situation you have no way of changing is a frightening thing.

My theology of intercession was entirely shot to pieces as a result of my childlessness. Before my prayers proved so catastrophically ineffective, I would have said to someone in my position that I did not know why God did not answer and that it was a painful mystery. But I would still have prayed and would have expected my prayers to have an effect. I do not pray in this way any more. I sometimes wonder why it made a difference going through it myself, since I already knew of so many instances where terrible things happened and God did not intervene – including in the lives of faithful, praying believers. But when it was my prayers that remained unanswered, I could no longer take refuge in mystery. I needed an explanation. If God did not always answer, then did God ever answer? Otherwise how could we explain the absurdity of God's choices, helping one person and not another? Rabbi Harold Kushner answers this question straightforwardly by letting go of God's omnipotence and keeping hold of God's love. The kind of prayer God answers, Kushner writes, is a prayer asking for the strength to get through whatever life throws at us (Kushner 1981, chapter 7). Kushner does not believe in miracles. Once my prayers had ended in disappointment, I found myself struggling to attribute a healing or a successful outcome to God. My thinking was, *If I praise God for that, I'll have to blame God for this.* I wasn't sure if my relationship with God could survive the knowledge that God could have helped me, but chose not to do so. And in this, I am not alone.[9]

The consolation

In Chapter 1, we considered several infertility narratives from the Old Testament, in which infertile women were eventually granted children when God heard their prayers. I suggested that these stories were ultimately alienating for people struggling with childlessness because, in each case, a miracle baby came along. There is another obvious difficulty with these stories, of course: they tell us that God can intervene, and that miracles occur when God does. In the Old Testament 'Control of [the womb] belongs neither to women nor to their husbands, neither to the fetus nor to society. Only God closes and opens wombs in judgment, in blessing, and in mystery' (Trible 1978, p. 35). This difficulty is not, of course, limited to people struggling with childlessness, but affects all those whose prayers remain unanswered – or, if you wish, all those whose prayers are answered 'no'.[10] Let us consider three unanswered prayers in the Bible.

For today's reader, the story of King David praying for his dying child is profoundly uncomfortable. David, the man after

God's own heart, has committed adultery and murder. He has conceived a child with Bathsheba and has had her husband killed. The prophet Nathan has challenged David on his actions and David has recognized his guilt. In 2 Samuel 12 we read:

David said to Nathan, 'I have sinned against the LORD.' Nathan said to David, 'Now the LORD has put away your sin; you shall not die. Nevertheless, because by this deed you have utterly scorned the LORD, the child that is born to you shall die.' Then Nathan went to his house.

The LORD struck the child that Uriah's wife bore to David, and it became very ill. David therefore pleaded with God for the child; David fasted, and went in and lay all night on the ground. The elders of his house stood beside him, urging him to rise from the ground; but he would not, nor did he eat food with them. On the seventh day the child died. And the servants of David were afraid to tell him that the child was dead; for they said, 'While the child was still alive, we spoke to him, and he did not listen to us; how then can we tell him the child is dead? He may do himself some harm.' But when David saw that his servants were whispering together, he perceived that the child was dead; and David said to his servants, 'Is the child dead?' They said, 'He is dead.'

Then David rose from the ground, washed, anointed himself, and changed his clothes. He went into the house of the LORD, and worshipped; he then went to his own house; and when he asked, they set food before him and he ate. Then his servants said to him, 'What is this thing that you have done? You fasted and wept for the child while it was alive; but when the child died, you rose and ate food.' He said, 'While the child was still alive, I fasted and wept; for I said, "Who knows? The LORD may be gracious to me, and the child may live." But now he is dead; why should I fast? Can I bring him back again? I shall go to him, but he will not return to me.' (2 Sam. 12.13–23)

In this story, it is clear that God could have spared David and Bathsheba's son, but chose not to do so. The explanation given is that David sinned against God by sleeping with a married woman and by having her husband killed. There is no consideration of the child himself, or of his mother, doubtless devastated at the death of her baby. This is a society in which women and children are the property of men, and seen in relation to their husbands and fathers. The sins of the husband and father are quite literally visited upon his family as well as upon himself.

This story of a child dying in a profoundly patriarchal society is very alien to twenty-first-century readers, and yet there is some resonance here for those of us who have been denied children. In this story, a passionate follower of the Lord prays earnestly, weeping and fasting, begging God that his baby might be spared. This is a man of true piety: he has sinned grievously, but these are prayers of faith. God does not answer, and the baby dies. This very harsh reality is lived by those of us who are not able to produce birth children, or who suffer the agony of miscarriage and stillbirth. We beg for God's mercy, and yet our children perish. In this story, David knew he had done wrong, and yet he did not quietly accept God's judgement upon his child. He did all he could to change God's mind. It was not enough. This is not a prayer 'answered, but not in the way he expected'. This prayer is not answered at all. Readers of the Bible may accept this harsh judgement in the context of David's behaviour: to teach him a lesson, perhaps, about holiness and the consequences of sin. And yet it is unlikely we would ever impose such a harsh interpretation on someone else's experience these days. No Christian with an ounce of humanity would tell a grieving parent that their loss was a punishment from God. This story is not comforting, but it presents the harsh realities with brutal clarity in a way that may be therapeutic, even cathartic. It unflinchingly demonstrates the problem faced by people whose babies have died, or whose babies will only ever exist in their imagination. It demands a response. People struggling with childlessness may well ask themselves whether, once all the euphemisms are swept away, this is what they are going through – God's refusal to save their child, despite their prayers.

There is another way in which this story may resonate with people struggling with childlessness: David cannot rest until all hope is gone. He refuses to eat or to change his clothes; he lies on the floor, praying, beseeching God to have mercy. He will not listen to anyone who tries to persuade him to get up off the ground or to take some food. His servants are surprised that, when he learns that his child is dead, he gets up, washes and eats a meal. David explains that he could not cease petitioning God until all hope was gone: 'While the child was still alive, I fasted and wept; for I said, "Who knows? The LORD may be gracious to me, and the child may live"' (2 Sam. 12.22). Now that there is no hope, however, he can stop: 'But now he is dead; why should I fast? Can I bring him back again? I shall go to him, but he will not return to me' (2 Sam. 12.23).

It is unthinkable that David should give up praying and fasting while there is still hope that God might intervene. Once the baby dies, however, there is nothing more he can do. This story does not, I think, imply that David has forgotten his child so quickly. Instead, it shows that, rather than simply expressing his emotions, David was doing all he could to save his son. This is the only power he can exercise in this situation, in this time long before medical science provided effective interventions for childhood illness. The frantic prayers and petitions can only stop once all hope has gone that they might be effective.

It can be very difficult for people going through fertility treatment to draw a line and say, 'no more', because there is almost always hope. So often they do not experience the brutal finality that King David did when his child died, an externally imposed ending. Generally, people have to decide for themselves when to stop trying. It is rare that a medical professional can tell someone that they have no hope of conceiving a child. There is almost always a treatment that can be offered that holds the possibility of a baby, however slight. Indeed, this can be the cruellest part of the experience of infertility: the inability to give up, grieve and heal because of the possibility that the next treatment cycle might work.[11] My husband and I talked about having three cycles of IVF – the number recommended by the National Institute for Health and Care Excellence (NICE) –

and then drawing a line. We would have had to pay for our third cycle, had we decided to go ahead. Because I responded so poorly to IVF, it was very clear after two cycles that there was no point in carrying on. Even at the time, I was aware that there was a sense in which this was a mercy. It was not a difficult decision because the odds of success were clearly so small. Most people going through unsuccessful fertility treatment will have to make the agonizing decision to stop at some point, knowing that – in theory – there is still hope.

One BBC interviewee recounted the break-up of his marriage due to his wife's determination to continue treatment: a determination that ultimately became self-destructive.[12] The toll that fertility treatment takes – on the body; on the emotions; on relationships between partners, as well as their relationships with family and friends – can be considerable. Katy suffered for years from chronic pelvic pain, finally receiving a diagnosis of endometriosis while trying to conceive in her early thirties. After four years of trying unsuccessfully to conceive, including one failed round of IVF, she realized that the emotional and physical cost of the treatment was just too high:

> It really does take so much from you, and the longer it went on, the more it was taking. And so I just got to this place where, you know, for my mental health, for my physical health, for my relationships, I just decided that the best path for me was to walk away from infertility without a baby and start to put that energy back into rebuilding my life and deciding what I wanted it to look like without a kid. (Katy, *Infertile AF*, 29 January 2020)

Encouraged by her husband and her therapist, Katy took the decision to prioritize her health and to have a hysterectomy. Following the surgery, her chronic pain was improved to the point where she was able to exercise and to plan trips away from home without worry for the first time in her life. She has no regrets.[13]

The story of David's unanswered prayer provides little comfort, but it does perhaps offer companionship. People struggling with childlessness may identify with David's desperation – his determination to do all he possibly can to save his child. They may well wonder why God fails to answer his prayers as well as their own. In all probability, they will find the biblical writer's explanation – that David had sinned – unsatisfying. An example of unanswered prayer that may offer a more palatable explanation is found in 2 Corinthians, where the apostle Paul writes of his 'thorn in the flesh':

> But if I wish to boast, I will not be a fool, for I will be speaking the truth. But I refrain from it, so that no one may think better of me than what is seen in me or heard from me, even considering the exceptional character of the revelations. Therefore, to keep me from being too elated, a thorn was given to me in the flesh, a messenger of Satan to torment me, to keep me from being too elated. Three times I appealed to the Lord about this, that it would leave me, but he said to me, 'My grace is sufficient for you, for power is made perfect in weakness.' So, I will boast all the more gladly of my weaknesses, so that the power of Christ may dwell in me. Therefore I am content with weaknesses, insults, hardships, persecutions, and calamities for the sake of Christ; for whenever I am weak, then I am strong. (2 Cor. 12.6–10)

Paul's prayers for the removal of his 'thorn in the flesh' were also answered 'no'. We do not know what Paul's affliction was – some kind of physical or psychiatric illness, perhaps. His understanding was that God allowed him to become ill – or made him ill – in order to keep him humble. This, perhaps, is the 'bigger plan' that, we are told, explains so many unanswered prayers. Harold Kushner acknowledges the many ways in which his son's short life and early death have made him a better rabbi:

> I am a more sensitive person, a more effective pastor, a more sympathetic counselor because of Aaron's life and death than I would ever have been without it. And I would give up all of those gains in a second if I could have my son back. If

I could choose, I would forgo all the spiritual growth and depth which has come my way because of our experiences, and be what I was fifteen years ago, an average rabbi, an indifferent counselor, helping some people and unable to help others, and the father of a bright, happy boy. But I cannot choose. (Kushner 1981, chapter 8)

There are many profound things God can do in a person's faith and character when they have endured great suffering. There is a difference, however, between asserting this truth and declaring that the personal faith development is part of God's 'bigger plan'. We can affirm that God uses suffering without declaring that God causes it. Indeed, the notion that God might cause such terrible suffering for the purposes of faith and character development is, to me, deeply offensive.

Rather than focusing on the notion that God allowed Paul to suffer for his improvement, perhaps it is Paul's reflections on weakness that may offer greater help. People struggling with childlessness have come face to face with their own weakness – their inability to create the future for which they long. They simply do not have the power to change a situation that is causing them so much pain. Theologians who have reflected upon disability, including those who are themselves disabled, understand only too well the illusion of strength and power that can all too easily be stripped away. Jean Vanier – some of whose weaknesses have sadly become all too well known since his death – reminds us that strength and power is only ever a temporary condition: 'Our lives are a mystery of growth from weakness to weakness, from the weakness of the little baby to the weakness of the aged. Throughout our lives, we are prone to fatigue, sickness, and accidents. Weakness is at the heart of each one of us.'[14]

Disability theologian Nancy Eiesland refers to those of us who do not have a recognized disability as 'temporarily able-bodied' persons (Eiesland 1994, p. 24). Strength, vitality and fertility are all temporary states. Those of us who live to old age; those of us who experience disability or chronic illness; those of us who experience involuntary childlessness:

we all have to come to terms with the limits of our power. Perhaps people struggling with childlessness have been given the (unwanted) gift of this stripping away of the illusion of potency.

We may be weak – we may even accept our weakness – but we often expect God to be strong. We sing of the greatness of God Almighty. Some of us were taught as children that God has 'the whole world in his hands'. The top 100 hymns, according to a 2013 survey by BBC *Songs of Praise*, includes many favourites that speak of God's mighty power. 'How Great Thou Art', 'Praise to the Lord, the Almighty, the King of creation' are favourites among those who favour traditional worship; 'How Great is our God' and 'King of Kings, Majesty' are favoured by those who prefer a worship band. The Christian Copyright Licensing International top 100 songs gives an insight into those songs most projected on to screens on Sunday mornings. It includes 'Mighty to Save', 'Lord Reign in Me' and 'The Lion and the Lamb'.[15] It may be hard to worship God as mighty King, however, when we feel the King has not heard our pleas or used their kingly power on our behalf. It may be difficult to worship the King of creation when our bodies remain barren.

Another song that made the BBC *Songs of Praise* top 100 portrays a different God, however. The 1983 Graham Kendrick song 'The Servant King' is still popular in many churches. This song represents God in humility, vulnerability, even weakness. In Chapter 2 we considered Christ's total identification with human pain, and even with death. As well as taking on our pain, Christ also took on our weakness. When considering the inaction of God in the face of my suffering, I have found myself contemplating God's deliberate self-emptying in the incarnation, God's surrender to cruelty and to helplessness on the cross. It is easier for me to worship the vulnerable, weak, powerless lamb than it is to contemplate the almighty King who has not protected me from disaster. Kevin Ellis contemplates the impotence of God, reflecting that many people would feel cheated or even alarmed at this possibility. And yet, the God of power can be alienating for those of us struggling with childlessness (Ellis 2013, pp. 141–3): 'when God is portrayed as all-powerful, all knowing and ever present, then there is little room for weakness, particularly among those who are supposed to be fashioned in the divine image. After all, who would countenance an impotent God?' (Ellis 2003, p. 13).

Ellis writes powerfully of the taboo of male impotence, which he sensed intuitively as a ten-year-old when a male doctor refused to meet his eye. He was born with a condition that impeded his fertility, and grasped on a deep level the unspeakableness of his condition from a young age. Even though I am female and experience a different set of taboos around fertility, when Ellis writes of 'searching for an impotent God', his words speak to me profoundly (Ellis 2003). And yet, even as I write, I fear the disapproval of others, as we who struggle with childlessness see our powerlessness reflected in the Godhead and have the audacity to say so. There is a fear of disrespecting God by attributing impotence to the Godhead. It is better for others if we carry the shame of our own powerlessness: God's honour, it seems, must be protected at all costs.

And yet, God did not protect God's honour on Good Friday. Christ suffered humiliation, powerlessness, terrible pain, and the ultimate weakness of death on the cross. When I contemplate Christ, our saviour, our example, the second Adam, I see power in operation mostly through weakness. When I contemplate the two great Christian festivals of Christmas and Easter, I see power at work through weakness. Christ emptying himself, taking on frail humanity, being born as a human baby. The Son of God humbling himself to be our Immanuel, God with us. At Easter, the Son takes on suffering and even death itself. The Lord says to the apostle Paul, 'power is made perfect in weakness' (2 Cor. 12.9). In context, Paul understands this as the declaration that God's power will be more clearly seen through Paul's weakness. Where there is less of Paul's competence, health and vigour to be seen, Christ can be seen more clearly. Applied more broadly, however, it seems to me that God's power is most often at work through weakness – that God seems to choose to operate mostly through weakness. God saves humanity through taking on weakness and submitting to the ultimate weakness of death – and, in this way, achieves the great victory of the resurrection. We who struggle with childlessness may be far from seeing the triumph of resurrection through our weakness. While the apostle Paul shows Christ at work more clearly through his weakness, in contrast, we may feel that our witness to the power of Christ at work in us is undermined by our suffering. At my lowest moments, I have never felt myself to be a very good model of the Christian life. Far from being patient in affliction, I was crushed by it; far from submitting to the divine will, I raged against it, ultimately coming to the conclusion that my childlessness was not something willed by God. And yet, in contemplating the God who chooses to be overpowered, crushed, abandoned and killed, I find a companion. I am no longer alone in my impotence. My impotence is made holy.

We have considered the powerlessness felt by people struggling with childlessness, and considered the weakness, even impotence, of God. We turn now to the issue of faith and trust. What does it mean to trust God when we have been so badly let down? What do we mean when we exhort people to 'trust God'? In Psalm 31 we read of a person in great distress, who has seen God save in the past, and declares their trust that God will do so again. Verses 1–2 beg for God's help:

> In you, O LORD, I seek refuge;
>   do not let me ever be put to shame;
>   in your righteousness deliver me.
> Incline your ear to me;
>   rescue me speedily.
> Be a rock of refuge for me,
>   a strong fortress to save me. (Ps. 31.1–2)

Then we read words of trust, including words that Luke's Jesus speaks from the cross:

> Into your hand I commit my spirit;
>   you have redeemed me, O LORD, faithful God.
>
> You hate those who pay regard to worthless idols,
> but I trust in the LORD. (Ps. 31.5–6)

The contrast between 'those who pay regard to worthless idols' and those who trust in the Lord is clear. It seems that the psalmist has experienced God's help in the past, evidence that God can be trusted now:

> I will exult and rejoice in your steadfast love,
>> because you have seen my affliction;
>> you have taken heed of my adversities,
>> and have not delivered me into the hand of the enemy;
>> you have set my feet in a broad place. (Ps. 31.7–8)

And then, once again, the psalmist confusingly switches back to the present situation, from memories of past help to desperate pleas for help in the here and now. To me, verses 11–12 speak into the shame of childlessness:

> I am the scorn of all my adversaries,
> a horror to my neighbours,
> an object of dread to my acquaintances;
> those who see me in the street flee from me.
> I have passed out of mind like one who is dead;
> I have become like a broken vessel. (Ps. 31.11–12)

What does it mean to trust God when our life's circumstances have turned us into an 'object of dread' and we are desperate for deliverance? The psalmist seems sure that God will save once again. The wisdom literature often gives us this message, explicitly declaring that the wise, who trust in God, will enjoy God's favour:

> Trust in the LORD with all your heart, and do not rely on your own insight. In all your ways acknowledge him, and he will make straight your paths. (Prov. 3.5–6)

So often, however, this does not seem to be the case. Trust God, for people struggling with childlessness, *cannot* mean 'trust that God will sort everything out'. People going through fertility treatment know that there are no guarantees; they may even know that there are more failures than successes. People suffering the agony of recurrent miscarriage know that no one can promise them a successful pregnancy next time. People looking for a partner with whom to have children know that it may never happen. They cannot trust that God will grant them a baby. They have to find an alternative.

Perhaps, when we exhort each other to 'trust God' we mean, 'Trust that God knows what's best for you. Trust that God has a bigger plan.' Some well-meaning Christians who hear my story will doubtless make sense of my family's experiences by their ending in our decision to adopt. At the time of writing, my husband and I have been approved as adopters and are waiting to be matched with a child. Some will say that God prevented us from having biological children because God had a particular child in mind for us, and us for them. God knew what God was doing.

It might be a lovely story on the surface, but dig a little deeper and it does not look so good. It certainly is not a good plan. A much better plan would have been to have protected the child we will adopt from the early experiences that have prompted them to be taken into care. A much better plan would have spared them the trauma of being separated from their biological family and, later, from their foster family, to try to form a new family with strangers. This is not good planning. This is making the best of a terrible situation. Adoption is no one's Plan A. I do not mean that adoption is 'second best'. I simply mean that it is better for children to stay with their birth family if they possibly can, and local authorities do all they can to keep them there. Placing a child with an adoptive family can only ever be Plan B. Furthermore, parenting a traumatized child is not an option for everyone. And what about the people who cannot adopt?

When I was still trying to conceive, I had a prayerful refrain before I looked at the pregnancy testing stick. *Dear God, even if I'm not pregnant this month, I know it doesn't mean I won't ever be. And even if I never get pregnant naturally, we could have IVF. And even if we never get pregnant, we can always adopt. And even if we never have kids, it will be OK.* It was not so much a prayer as an attempt to guard against every possible eventuality. I felt, as a committed Christian, that I should be bringing this difficult experience before God. I wanted to 'trust God', but I knew that God might not answer my prayers. I was not so much talking to God as to myself – trying to convince myself that everything would be OK. Trying not to get too upset by the negative result. And yet, after 30 or so negative pregnancy tests and two rounds of IVF, everything was not OK. God did not seem to know what God was doing, and I became enraged whenever anyone tried to tell me that God could be trusted in this situation. Merryn, who went through IVF, a long and fruitless time on an adoption waiting list, more IVF, a phantom pregnancy and ultimate disappointment, asks: 'What can you really trust God for ... when you ask with all your heart and you're ignored?' (Voysey 2013, p. 16). Kristina felt suicidal after losing her twin girls at birth. In a letter to Elaine Tyler May she writes: 'Everyone said that they are in God's hands. I don't trust God with them – look what happened to me!' (Tyler May 1995, p. 239).

In her book *Living with Infertility*, Rosemary Morgan argues that putting our hope in God means believing that we will have reasons to praise God. Even if we are never blessed with children, we can still trust that we will be improved by God, blessed by God, that we will meet with God (Morgan 2013, p. 51). In other words, we might say that trusting God is trusting that God will give us good things in the future, even if God never grants the particular good thing that we are so desperately yearning for. This insight is a good start. I have found myself wondering, however, whether trusting God is actually much simpler – trusting in God's character. Trusting that God is good and loving, in the face of evidence to the contrary. Trusting that God cares. Trusting that God will always be there. Trusting that God can handle our most uncomfortable emotions. When I was at my most raw and disappointed, I felt many very ugly and deeply uncomfortable emotions. When I expressed some of my distress to people of faith, they often seemed to feel the need to defend God's honour by reminding me of God's goodness and trustworthiness. I wonder now whether God's trustworthiness lies partly in the very fact that God does not require that we tidy up our emotions or that we hide anything in prayer. I was blessed with some close friends and family members who were able to handle these emotions, some of whom are mentioned in the dedication of this book. Those people who helped me the most accepted even my ugliest emotions, and never tried to make me feel better.

Much later, when I started reading in preparation for adoption, I discovered the importance in child development of accepting and 'containing' children's emotions. Psychotherapist Philippa Perry explains that, although it may seem counterintuitive, it is by recognizing and accepting children's emotions, rather than 'shushing', that we help them to bear what they are feeling:

> When other people, especially our children, are unhappy, denying their difficult feelings is sometimes our default option. It can feel like the right thing to do. It might feel right to try to belittle, advise, distract or even scold the feelings out of them. We don't want the person we love to be unhappy, and being fully open to their unhappiness or their rage can feel dangerous and unsettling for us; it can even feel as if we are encouraging these feelings in some way. But when feelings are disallowed they do not disappear. They merely go into hiding, where they fester and cause trouble later on in life ...
>
> There is no guaranteed way to avoid mental-health difficulties, but it certainly helps to instil in us a belief that, whatever emotion we experience, we are still acceptable and, however bad we may feel, it will pass. (Perry 2019, p. 54)

Perhaps 'trusting God' could mean trusting that God will respond to our emotions with nurture rather than anger; with acceptance rather than judgement; with arms open wide. Perhaps we might trust that God can hold all we are feeling – can hold us – until we are better able to bear it. God then might become not the all-powerful parent who can make it all better, but the parent who is strong enough to cope with the tumult of our emotions, with the depths of our grief. Perhaps 'trust God' might then become an invitation to experience comfort, rather than a rebuke.

In Mark 9 we read of a prayer that was unanswered until Jesus intervened, and of a parent who had all but lost hope:

When they came to the disciples, they saw a great crowd around them, and some scribes arguing with them. When the whole crowd saw him, they were immediately overcome with awe, and they ran forward to greet him. He asked them, 'What are you arguing about with them?' Someone from the crowd answered him, 'Teacher, I brought you my son; he has a spirit that makes him unable to speak; and whenever it seizes him, it dashes him down; and he foams and grinds his teeth and becomes rigid; and I asked your disciples to cast it out, but they could not do so.' He answered them, 'You faithless generation, how much longer must I be among you? How much longer must I put up with you? Bring him to me.' And they brought the boy to him. When the spirit saw him, immediately it threw the boy into convulsions, and he fell on the ground and rolled about, foaming at the mouth. Jesus asked the father, 'How long has this been happening to him?' And he said, 'From childhood. It has often cast him into the fire and into the water, to destroy him; but if you are able to do anything, have pity on us and help us.' Jesus said to him, 'If you are able! – All things can be done for the one who believes.' Immediately the father of the child cried out, 'I believe; help my unbelief!' When Jesus saw that a crowd came running together, he rebuked the unclean spirit, saying to it, 'You spirit that keeps this boy from speaking and hearing, I command you, come out of him, and never enter him again!' After crying out and convulsing him terribly, it came out, and the boy was like a corpse, so that most of them said, 'He is dead.' But Jesus took him by the hand and lifted him up, and he was able to stand. When he had entered the house, his disciples asked him privately, 'Why could we not cast it out?' He said to them, 'This kind can come out only through prayer.' (Mark 9.14–29)

On the surface, this story serves simply to reinforce the problem: the Bible teaches us that God will answer when we persevere in prayer, and yet our experience often tells us otherwise. The father in the story has seen his son at the mercy of danger- ous convulsions since childhood and, in what sounds very like weary desperation, asks Jesus to do something 'if he can'. Jesus hears the doubt: this father has almost lost hope that anyone can do anything for his boy. Jesus challenges him – indeed, it sounds rather like a rebuke: 'All things can be done for the one who believes' (Mark 9.23). Perhaps we have heard this kind of rebuke from other Christians who are disturbed by the lack of faith to which our experiences drive us. Few are insensitive enough to tell those who are suffering that they do not have enough faith. But they may well insist that our prayers have been answered, just not in the way we wanted. Or that God sees a bigger picture that makes sense of our tragedy. Or that we must not allow our sorrow to cause us to be angry at God. This man's worry for his son seems to have worn away at his faith. And yet there is still some left: 'I believe; help my unbe- lief!' (Mark 9.24). There is both faith and doubt within him. He lives with the tension between what he sees before him and what he hopes for in faith.

Translations of Mark 9.24 that stick closely to the original Greek usually choose a version of the following:

> I do believe; help [me overcome] my unbelief. (Amplified Bible)

Translations and paraphrases that seek more straightforward English offer the following alternatives:

> I do have faith, but not enough. Help me have more! (Good News Bible)

> I believe. Help me with my doubts! (*The Message*)

Is faith something that is quantifiable – of which we can have more or less? Or is it in direct contrast with unbelief – a choice of one or the other, belief or unbelief (despite the fact that the parent in the story has both)? Or should we use the softer language of doubts, plural (rather than doubt, singular, sometimes seen as the enemy of faith)? We can have faith while entertaining doubts: questions that seek to undermine our faith.

There are a number of possibilities, and yet I think we all instinctively understand the mixture of faith and doubt in this man's heart. Jesus has earlier expressed frustration with the lack of faith he is seeing – 'You faithless generation, how much longer must I be among you? How much longer must I put up with you?' (Mark 9.19). And yet, wonderfully, Jesus accepts this half-hearted, weary and partial declaration of faith. He does help. Finally, this man's prayer is answered. Although most of us will not have such a dramatic divine intervention, and many of us will remain wearily disappointed, there is nevertheless assurance in this story that God accepts the scraps of faith we have left. Jesus seems to accept that it is possible both to trust and to be deeply sceptical. And that in itself is a reason to trust him.

The practice

Over the past few years I have become a little obsessed by the question: What do we mean when we tell one another to 'trust God'? Whenever anyone says it to me, it sounds as if they are telling me to stop doubting and believe that everything will be OK. They are telling me that God is in control. They want to see quiet resignation and simple faith in the face of adversity: the kind of simple faith that waits patiently for God to answer my prayers – only God has not answered them.

I would like to suggest that we try to finish this sentence. When we exhort one another to 'trust God', I wonder if it might help to name what we are trusting God *for*? I wonder if we need to dig a little deeper to discover what it means to 'trust God' while living out a story that does not seem to be heading for a happy ending. By finishing the sentence, we expose what it is we are actually saying – and can ask ourselves whether we really believe it. By devising new ways of finishing the sentence, instead of piling on the pressure, we might inspire one another to imagine what it might mean to trust God when there is no ending – when there may *never* be an ending:

When we are secure and the world is orderly, 'trust God' means:	When we are powerless and weak, 'trust God' might mean:
Trust that God is in control	Trust that God is with you
Trust that God will deliver you	Trust that God cares
Trust that God is good	Trust that God has not forgotten what it is to suffer alone
Trust that everything will work out	Trust that God still loves you
Trust that everything happens for a reason, according to God's will	Trust that God can bring resurrection, even into your desperate situation
Trust that God will not give you more than you can handle	Trust that God can hold all your emotions, even the ugly ones
Trust that God knows better than you	Trust that God will help you bear it
Trust that God sees the bigger picture	Trust that God sees you

As we discover what it is to trust God from a place of struggle, I would love to hear more stories told that do not have happy endings. Testimonies given from the front of church, and stories written in blogs and Christian magazines, speak of miraculous answers to prayer, while those whose prayers remain unanswered usually stay silent. In episode 45 of Ali Prato's podcast *Infertile AF*, we hear Katy's story. Katy had got in touch to say that she hoped Ali would interview more people whose infertility stories did not end with a baby. Ali's explanation is interesting: she says that this is not by design. She has not chosen to edit out stories of permanent infertility, but it seems that people are happier to talk about their infertility once they are in a position of strength, having had the longed-for baby.[16] And what is true of an infertility podcast is also true of the Church. It is easier and more palatable to tell stories that have ended in success.

Lizzie Lowrie and her friend Sheila Matthews started the excellent blog *Saltwater and Honey* along with their husbands, Dave and Elis, because they wanted to tell their stories 'from the middle'. In her memoir, published in 2020, Lowrie explains that all the infertility blogs they found, whether written by Christians or not, were either very bitter or written from the perspective of a happy ending with a 'rainbow baby'. They believe that stories with happy endings are not the only ones that are worth telling (Lowrie 2020, pp. 227–8). For Lowrie, this battle to tell her story and to have it received as valid continues. In a post from March 2016, she describes being interviewed by Sky TV about some new research into recurrent miscarriage. She was told she came across well, but her interview was not shown. It was cut in favour of an interview with a woman whose tragedy had ultimately ended with the joy of a baby. Lowrie's blog post is written in the form of an open letter to Sky TV: '... by replacing me with a woman and her baby it felt like you were saying her story was better than mine and that's an opinion I've been fighting for years'.[17]

In the final chapter of her memoir, published in 2020, Lowrie describes a more recent, less public rejection. She and her husband were put in touch with a couple who were themselves wrestling with recurrent miscarriage, and trying to make sense of it in the light of their faith. Lizzie explains that her husband sent a link to the blog so as to introduce their story, accompanied by an offer to meet and chat in person. The other husband wrote back to turn down the offer of a meeting, as his wife had found their story too upsetting. A tale of six devastating miscarriages, with no medical explanation and no miracle baby or adopted child, was not what this lady wanted to hear. Perhaps she wanted to hear about a couple whose prayers had eventually been answered; who had ultimately, after many disappointments and much waiting, been offered a medical treatment that had enabled Lizzie to carry a baby to term. Perhaps, at the very least, she had wanted a set of neat and comforting answers. But Lizzie is too honest for that. In a post from 2018 she admits that her prayer life is 'still deeply fractured', nine years after her first miscarriage.[18] Kevin Ellis is also one half of a clergy couple whose infertility proved to be permanent, although he and his wife have since adopted a child. He argues that stories that do not have a happy ending also need to be 'embraced as holy' (Ellis 2006, p. 13): 'Not everything in the world is clear-cut and simple to explain; as long as Christians believe that the world is easy to understand, simple flat-pack answers will be the order of the day, and there will therefore be those – like those who are childless – who are permitted only to hover on the fringes of the church' (Ellis 2006, p. 21).

We have to encourage one another to tell our stories, including – or perhaps especially – those that are troubling and that do not end with a successful outcome. This kind of storytelling will look different in a Roman Catholic congregation than in a charismatic evangelical fellowship, but is equally important in both. In some traditions it will be natural and appropriate for someone to stand up and tell their story during public worship; in others, this kind of testimony may work better in a small group setting (and, indeed, this is likely to be much less intimidating for the one telling their story). Stories can also be shared through newsletters and pastoral updates. I received permission to use a friend's story of severe mental illness in written form. She wrote a very honest account of her struggles, without giving away any details that would identify her, and was happy for me to give out paper copies of her story during a discussion-based service exploring mental health. It is also crucial, I believe, that church leaders are prepared to be among the first to share. American speaker, writer and pastor Nadia Bolz-Weber speaks of the importance of vulnerability as creating a space for others to tell their stories. She calls this form of leadership, 'Screw it, I'll go first'.[19] If leaders are not prepared to be vulnerable, they cannot expect their congregations to open up.

The three-day event of cross, grave and resurrection can be seen as a story with a happy ending. Alan Lewis explains that we, who know how the story ends, skip from cross to empty tomb, dealing with the horror of Christ's death by rushing to his resurrection. Lewis reminds us, however, of the simple fact that the first followers of Jesus did not know what was coming. They had to deal with their grief and disappointment, their sense of injustice and perhaps hopelessness, with no idea of the miracle that was coming. If we rush too quickly to the end: 'we may suppress the very good news which the story holds for men and women who have to endure life slowly and patiently, who hear no answers to their own questions, or experience tensions with no guarantee of eventual resolution' (Lewis 2001, p. 30).

However these stories are shared, their power is immense. This level of honesty, openness and vulnerability enables all of us to see our struggles and our unanswered questions as holy. Through this kind of truth-telling we can begin to see that we are not alone, to accept our stories as they are, and to work out what it means to have faith in the midst of painful struggle.

Notes

1 In 2018, British IVF patients had a birth rate of 23 per cent per embryo transferred. See: '2018 trends in fertility treatment', *Human Fertilisation & Embryology Authority*, www.hfea.gov.uk/about-us/news-and-press-releases/2020-news-and-press-releases/2018-trends-in-fertility-treatment/, accessed 1.8.2020.

2 '2018 trends in fertility treatment.'

3 The Miscarriage Association, 'Miscarriage', Miscarriage Association, www.miscarriageassociation.org.uk/information/miscarriage/, accessed 17.1.2021.

4 The National Institute for Health and Care Excellence (NICE) recommends three fresh cycles of IVF be offered to people needing this treatment to conceive. In his excellent book *The Essential Fertility Guide*, Dr Robert Winston expresses the cruelty of the postcode lot-

tery which means that a full course of treatment offering a reasonable chance of success is only offered to the lucky few. See Winston 2015, chapter 1.

5 Jean Twenge recommends that women aged 35–39 go to see a doctor after six months of trying to get pregnant and women over 40 after three months. See Twenge 2012, p. 184.

6 Comments made in an interview on the Ali Prato podcast *Infertile AF*, episode 18 (18 July 2019).

7 Trolice quotes these statistics in his *Infertile AF* interview.

8 Twenge 2012, chapter 6. Twenge cites two studies, one of which found that 78 per cent of women who were trying to get pregnant aged 35–39 were pregnant within a year; in the other study, it was 82 per cent.

9 See, for example: Lizzie Lowrie, 2018, 'What happened when I stopped asking', *Saltwater and Honey*, 11 March, http://saltwaterand honey.org/blog/what-happened-when-i-stopped-asking, accessed 7.3. 2021.

10 Some declare that God answers all prayers, but that some are answered 'no'. In my opinion, this makes little difference. It is no easier to explain why God answers 'no' than to explain why God does not answer at all.

11 See, for example, Tyler May 1995, p. 224.

12 Interview with Katy featured in episode 45 (29 January 2020) of Ali Prato's podcast *Infertile AF*, https://infertileaf.libsyn.com

13 Interview with Katy featured in episode 45 (29 January 2020) of Ali Prato's podcast *Infertile AF*, https://infertileaf.libsyn.com.

14 Vanier 1998, p. 39. A report published since Vanier's death in 2019 shockingly revealed that he had manipulative and abusive sexual relationships with six women throughout his long ministry.

15 '2013: The UK's Top 100 Hymns', BBC One *Songs of Praise*, www.bbc.co.uk/programmes/articles/42TSJoLNMfpohowNvxql-w93/2013-the-uks-top-100-hymns; 'CCLI Top 100', *SongSelect*, https:// songselect.ccli.com/search/results?List=top100, accessed 21.1.2021.

16 Ali Prato, *Infertile AF*, https://infertileaf.libsyn.com

17 Lizzie Lowrie, 2016, 'Rejected by Sky TV', *Saltwater and Honey*, 16 March, http://saltwaterandhoney.org/blog/rejected-by-sky-tv, accessed 23.8.2016.

18 Lowrie, 'What happened when I stopped asking'.

19 From a talk at Greenbelt that I attended in 2018.

4

Barren

Three things are never satisfied;
 four never say, 'Enough':
Sheol, the barren womb,
 the earth ever thirsty for water,
 and the fire that never says, 'Enough.'
(Prov. 30.15b–16)

The experience

One of the very lowest points of my struggle with childlessness came as I was sitting in an IVF clinic in recovery after my
second egg collection. IVF involves artificially stimulating the
ovaries and then harvesting a large number of eggs, which are
collected during a surgical procedure. For optimum success,
an IVF cycle requires 10–14 eggs. These eggs are mixed with
sperm, with the hope of creating several embryos. Not all eggs
fertilize; not all fertilized eggs develop into viable embryos;
not all embryos survive for transfer; most transferred embryos
do not implant.[1] IVF therefore needs a good number of eggs
because possible embryos are lost at every stage. During the
preparation for my first cycle of IVF, a blood test revealed
that I was likely to need a fairly high dose of hormones to get
enough eggs for treatment. Unfortunately, my body responded
very poorly to ovarian stimulation, and I was put on the very
highest dose of the follicle stimulating hormones in order to get
the best possible response.

   At my first egg collection, they got just three eggs. After that
cycle failed, my consultant put me on a different drug regimen,
on a very high dose of hormones, with the hope of getting a
better response. I arrived for my second egg collection feeling

hopeful. The procedure is carried out under sedation: you are groggy, but conscious and can hear and understand what is said. The embryologists count out loud as they find the microscopic eggs, and so you therefore know straight away how the procedure has gone. I heard someone say, 'We got one', and then the procedure finished and I was helped off the operating table and into a wheelchair to be taken to recovery. I remember thinking, *Why are you stopping? You only got one.* I knew enough about IVF by that point to realize that our chances of success had just shrunk to nearly zero.

As I sat in recovery, sipping my restorative cup of tea and staring brokenly at the floor, I was aware of couples to our left and right. The only privacy each of us had was a curtain screening us from each other. I heard someone to my left ask the nurse: 'They got nine eggs – is that good?' and I broke down in tears. My husband leapt up from his chair to console me, and knocked my teacup to the floor. A very small part of me registered the slapstick humour in the situation. The nurse pulled aside the curtain and asked what was wrong. *They got one egg, that's what's bloody wrong*, I thought, but did not say. My husband is more observant than I am (and was not recovering from sedation) and he later told me he'd overheard the couple to our right discussing their treatment – they were having ICSI. Intra-cytoplasmic sperm injection is a procedure that is sometimes necessary when the man's sperm is unable to penetrate and fertilize the egg. A tiny needle is used to help the sperm penetrate the egg to create an embryo. It's a procedure that is fiddly, and more expensive than standard IVF. Those of us sitting in the clinic that morning represented the wide variety of experiences that exist even among people undergoing fertility treatment. Some enjoy the riches of nine eggs; others struggle to produce enough eggs for treatment; still others have sperm that need help to do what most sperm can do naturally.

Not all people want to have children, but most assume that they will be able to do so if and when they choose. As soon as we hit puberty in our early teens we are, in theory, fertile. Coming to the realization that your body cannot do what most others can do easily can be a very bitter experience. I found myself drawn to the word 'barren'. This is a word that I would find highly offensive should anyone else apply it to me, and yet claiming the word myself felt fitting and appropriate. It is a word that captures the profound hopelessness I experience in the face of my body's inability to nurture life. It is a word that stares that reality in the face. Barren makes me think of a desert landscape in which nothing is growing – there is no life. Childlessness can make life feel barren for a time. The word 'barren' is more usually applied to women, but men also feel the pain of childlessness keenly. Dave uses the word 'sterile' to express his hopelessness: 'I was sterile, and sterile is a for-ever thing, with nothing to look forward to! ... The hurt and the mind-numbing pain ... doesn't ever go away' (Tyler May 1995, p. 1).

Knowing that your body is never going to be able to bring forth new life can make everything seem pretty pointless: your relationship, and indeed your whole life, at a dead end (Spring 1989, p. 4). Some people mourn babies who died through mis-carriage or stillbirth. Others mourn babies who will never be. A future that will never happen. A hope that seems so very nat-ural and reasonable, and yet is forever frustrated. For a time, I felt as if nothing good was ever going to happen. Perhaps it was because I had been disappointed so many times.

While researching her book on the history of childlessness in America, Elaine Tyler May received over 500 letters from people relating their experiences of childlessness, whether voluntary or involuntary. She found that childless people share 'the stigma and isolation of being nonparents in a pronatal society'. Wishing for children, while being unable to have them, in a society where almost everyone else can and does, and wonders why you do not. Many of those who wrote to Tyler May expressed their anger at 'rude and intrusive' questions and comments. It is not uncommon, for example, to hear those who are parents make the remark that people cannot really know love until they have children. Doubtless people never intend this to be a pointed barb, but it cuts deep.

It is quite common for people to joke about fertility. 'He only has to look at his wife and she's pregnant.' Sometimes babies come along 'by accident'. For those of us who cannot have children, not being able to do what others can do with so little effort is not only frustrating, but deeply shaming. I was surprised how much it hurt when my consultant told me my AMH level – indicating ovarian reserve – was low. Of course, it is not something I caused, or can do anything about, just as those who seem to be super-fertile are like that by chance rather than virtue. And yet infertility is a physical condition for which people can feel deep shame. We have already considered the strange silence of the fertility clinic, in which no one speaks or even makes eye contact, and the isolation – sometimes self-imposed – of childless people. The silence and the isolation are, I think, driven partly by shame.

Some have drawn parallels between infertility and disability, and there is a sense in which people who cannot conceive, or whose pregnancies end in miscarriage, are disabled (Moss and Baden 2015, p. 4). Infertility is both a highly visible and an invisible disability (Moss and Baden 2015, p. 7). Nancy Eiesland defines a disability as 'a form of inability or limitation in performing roles or tasks expected of an individual within a social environment' (Eiesland 1994, p. 27). A woman who is unable to conceive and bear children, or a man who is unable to father a child, despite wishing to do so, cannot do something most others can: a limitation in creating the future they wish for.[2] Furthermore, a person experiencing infertility lives in a social environment in which it is expected that all adults will find a partner and have children. We tend to speculate (against our better nature) as to the reasons why a person is 'still single' once they reach a certain age, or why a couple who have been together for some years remain childless. These speculations are often experienced by single and childless people as offensive and intrusive when they are voiced.

Eiesland distinguishes between 'impairment', 'disability' and 'handicap' in ways that are extremely helpful when considering infertility. She defines an impairment as an abnormality: 'a loss of physiological form or function'. A disability is 'an inability to perform some task or activity considered necessary' because of an impairment. Finally, Eiesland defines a handicap as a social disadvantage resulting from the above. An impairment does not necessarily lead to a disability, and a disability need not be a handicap (Eiesland 1994, p. 27). A person experiencing infertility may have a specific medical impairment, such as poor-quality sperm or quantity of sperm in the case of a man, or blocked fallopian tubes in the case of a woman. These factors do not necessarily make conceiving a child impossible, but it may well be more difficult, just as a person with limited mobility may well be able to walk, but may find it harder to do so than their peers. If a person with a reproductive impairment is unable to father or to bear a child as a result of their impairment, they may experience the disability of infertility – an inability to perform the task of having children, a task that they may well consider necessary, just as the society around them considers it to be necessary. Finally, a social disadvantage may arise from this inability to procreate.

Applying Eiesland's analysis to the experience of infertility highlights the complexities of a diagnosis of infertility as well as the social context in which it takes place. A person who experiences infertility – the failure of conception after one year of trying – may well conceive a child eventually. There is usually some treatment that can be offered that holds the possibility of conceiving a child, however small. There is so much that can be done to prevent the reproductive impairment from resulting in the permanent 'disability' of infertility. And while some people's impairments do mean that they are never able to have a child, we can also see that the disability of infertility need not result in a handicap – a social disadvantage.

Infertility is a disabling condition that has social consequences, and greater understanding and awareness of infertility could lessen the social disadvantage. There is a deep personal pain, however, for women and men who are unable to create new life. There is so much joy that surrounds pregnancy and early childhood – along with much pain, as most new parents are quick to point out – and it can seem that a childless life will be a joyless one.

The consolation

In Chapter 1 we considered a number of stories from Scripture where infertile couples are blessed with miracle children. In the Bible, almost without exception, infertility is seen as a curse – a sign that God's blessing has been withheld. While there are single people such as Elijah and Elisha, the apostle Paul, and of course Jesus himself, who are single and childless in the Bible, there are no stories of faithful couples without children.[3] We even find an example of someone who is apparently cursed with childlessness as a result of her cynical lack of devotion to God (see the story of Michal in 2 Samuel 6.16, 20–23).

The covenant promise, as understood in the Old Testament, includes the reward of fruitful wombs for those who obey the Lord. In the promised land, everyone is fertile:

No one shall miscarry or be barren in your land. (Ex. 23.26)

If you heed these ordinances, by diligently observing them, the LORD your God will maintain with you the covenant loyalty that he swore to your ancestors; he will love you, bless you, and multiply you; he will bless the fruit of your womb and the fruit of your ground, your grain and your wine and your oil, the increase of your cattle and the issue of your flock, in the land that he swore to your ancestors to give you. You shall be the most blessed of peoples, with neither sterility nor barrenness among you or your livestock. The LORD will turn away from you every illness; all the dread diseases of Egypt that you experienced, he will not inflict on you, but he will lay them on all who hate you. (Deut. 7.12–15)

Those of us who cannot have children have no place in the land flowing with milk and honey. Our experiences sit uneasily beside the wonderful promises made to the people of God. We have been shut out of the blessing that has been spoken over Israel. Infertility has no place among faithful followers of the Lord. This understanding of fruitfulness for the faithful is also found in the biblical wisdom tradition. Children are a sign of

God's blessing. Those who love God and are loved by God are fruitful. In the Psalms we read:

> Happy is everyone who fears the LORD,
>   who walks in his ways.
> You shall eat the fruit of the labour of your hands;
>   you shall be happy, and it shall go well with you.
>
> Your wife will be like a fruitful vine
>   within your house;
> your children will be like olive shoots
>   around your table.
> Thus shall the man be blessed
>   who fears the LORD. (Ps. 128.1–4)

And in Proverbs:

> Grandchildren are the crown of the aged,
>   and the glory of children is their parents. (Prov. 17.6)

The isolation and shame of those who are struggling with childlessness are simply compounded by texts such as these. We have been denied the children who are a sign of God's blessing: the unspoken implication is that we are under God's curse. We have not been granted the fruitfulness that is the promise made to those who obey God's covenant – so perhaps we are being punished for our unfaithfulness? Doubtless few preachers would declare this from the pulpit, and few pastors offer this explanation to troubled people in their care. Nevertheless, there is little to comfort and much to alienate childless people from the community of faith here – and perhaps even from God. What have we done to miss out on the blessing everyone else enjoys?

The wisdom tradition includes texts that seem to challenge this neat view of the world, however. Set against the simplistic worldview of Proverbs, in which the wise and faithful prosper and the foolish and ungodly perish, we have Job and Ecclesiastes. In Job, we have a righteous person who does suffer greatly: he loses all his property, and then his children are killed. While Job's comforters seek to convince him that he must have done something to anger the Almighty, in fact we as readers know that this is not the case. Job is being tested, but not as a result of any sin on his part. At the end of the book, after much lament by Job, and many self-righteous platitudes by Job's friends, God shows up. God's answer to Job's complaints could be paraphrased: 'Where were you when I made the world?' Job offers a degree of comfort when we experience painful struggle. We may hear our own complaints spoken by Job, and hear echoes of the unhelpful things others have said to us in the words of Job's friends. There is even a bleak kind of comfort in the words spoken by God – words that remind us that God is above and beyond; that God sees and does more than we can imagine; that we are creatures and God is our creator. And yet the book ends with Job's fortunes restored, and more children born to him – as if these will simply replace the children he has lost. As a person experiencing childlessness, I find greater resonances in Ecclesiastes.

The Teacher of Ecclesiastes goes even further than the book of Job in challenging received wisdom. In Ecclesiastes, all those who face disappointment and senseless suffering find company, no easy answers are forthcoming, and God does not make an appearance. The Teacher declares that everything is 'vanity'. The Hebrew word *hebel*, traditionally translated 'vanity', occurs 34 times in Ecclesiastes compared with 34 occurrences in the whole of the rest of the Old Testament (Whybray 1989, p. 63). Unfortunately, this important word is very difficult to render reliably in English and translators of the Bible have opted for a wide variety of different possibilities. The NRSV favours the traditional 'vanity' whereas the NIV and NLT prefer 'meaningless'; other possibilities include 'nothingness', 'worthlessness', 'futility', 'mystery' and 'impermanence' (Whybray 1989, p. 64); to which Fox adds 'ephemerality', 'incomprehensibility', 'senselessness' and 'absurd' (Fox 1999, pp. 28–9). The word *hebel* is often coupled with *rĕ'ût/ra'yon rûah*, meaning 'shepherding', 'chasing after' or 'feeding on' wind or air. The biblical paraphrase in *The Message* cleverly reflects the root meaning of *hebel*, which is vapour: 'I've seen it all and it's nothing but smoke – smoke, and spitting into the wind' (Eccles. 1.14). There are a considerable number of possible meanings, and it is difficult to know what to make of them. Was the Teacher emphasizing our mortality, that life was short – hence, 'impermanence' or 'ephemerality'? Was he trying to say that, since life is short, all our endeavours are pointless – in which case 'worthless' or 'futile' would fit better? Was he saying that the world could not be understood; that it was 'incomprehensible'? In Ecclesiastes we have a thinker whose view of the world is very different to that found in Proverbs – in fact, very different to the rest of the biblical canon. To those who joyfully declare that God is good, those who follow God prosper, and the world makes sense, the Teacher declares: everything is meaningless. Life is short, incomprehensible, and pointless. These are strong statements indeed, and rather startling to find in the Bible. And yet, here they are.

To the many possible translations of *hebel*, I might add, 'barren'. The concept of barrenness expresses for me not simply my body's inability to conceive and nurture new life, but the profound desolation that inability has wreaked in every area of my existence. It seemed impossible for a time to find any substantial meaning in my life when I knew I would not have a baby. The heart of the Teacher's complaint is that good does not always win out, and anyway we all die in the end, so everything is *hebel*. My complaint with life was, and to an extent still is, that I cannot bring forth new life, I cannot create new people to love, and so everything is barren. Barren, for me, captures so many of the possible translations of *hebel*. I feel a sense of worthlessness, of 'less than', because I am childless. My life feels futile, because I will never have the joy of a baby, of nurturing and loving them and watching them grow up to have babies of their own. My life is perhaps even more impermanent and ephemeral than others because I will not be granted the genetic immortality of biological children. Where the Teacher declares, 'all is vanity', I declare, 'all is barren'.

There is a brief explicit reference in Ecclesiastes to childlessness:

Again, I saw vanity under the sun: the case of solitary individuals, without sons or brothers; yet there is no end to all their toil, and their eyes are never satisfied with riches. 'For whom am I toiling', they ask, 'and depriving myself of pleasure?' This also is vanity and an unhappy business. (Eccles. 4.7–8)

People who want children and cannot have them can find themselves wondering what, for them, is the point of all their hard work? Living in a house or flat with a spare room that remains unoccupied. Accumulating savings that they can only spend on themselves. Listening to others exclaiming that the most important thing in the world to them is their children, who give their lives its meaning. This is *hebel*, vanity, barren.

Another element of the vanity of life is its mystery – and the example given by the Teacher in Ecclesiastes has particular resonance for people experiencing infertility:

Just as you do not know how the breath comes to the bones in the mother's womb, so you do not know the work of God, who makes everything. (Eccles. 11.5)

This sums up the frustration I endured for years. Ultimately, there is nothing anyone can do to 'bring breath to the bones'. There is so much about fertility that is not well understood, and much that seems to be blind chance. Fertility clinics will grade the quality of embryos and tell people undergoing treatment that they are transferring a 'top quality' one, but these criteria are fairly arbitrary: no embryologist can tell by looking at the small group of cells that constitutes an embryo whether it is viable or not (Winston 2015, chapter 5). I paid £250 for a doctor to scratch the lining of my uterus because there is some research evidence that an embryo is more likely to implant after an 'endometrial scratch'. That may well be true, but it didn't work for me. There is a great deal of mystery that surrounds conception and it often feels like rolling dice.

The Teacher sees meaninglessness in the lives of those with children too:

There is an evil that I have seen under the sun, and it lies heavy upon humankind: those to whom God gives wealth, possessions, and honour, so that they lack nothing of all that they desire, yet God does not enable them to enjoy these things, but a stranger enjoys them. This is vanity; it is a grievous ill. A man may beget a hundred children, and live many years; but however many are the days of his years, if he does not enjoy life's good things, or has no burial, I say that a stillborn child is better off than he. For it comes into vanity and goes into darkness, and in darkness its name is covered; moreover, it has not seen the sun or known anything; yet it finds rest rather than he. Even though he should live a thousand years twice over, yet enjoy no good – do not all go to one place? (Eccles. 6.1–6)

Even if we are blessed with wealth and family, if we are not able to enjoy these things while we have them then our lives remain meaningless. Here we encounter the stark, disturbing image of a stillborn child, more fortunate than the man with 'a hundred children' who takes no joy in life, according to the Teacher in Ecclesiastes. Life is so barren, so devoid of meaning, that the one who is never born is fortunate compared with the living. We also encounter once again a recurring theme: everyone dies in the end, so what is the point? People often try to counter mortality through legacy, leaving their genetic inheritance in their children. And yet, even in a culture where children were a sign of God's blessing and crucial for providing for old age, the Teacher is unconvinced.

Ecclesiastes is a strange kind of comfort but, for me, it is a comfort. It is a book that names the uncomfortable realities of life, the great taboo of death, declares that everything is meaningless, and reaches no neat conclusions. The only answer that the Teacher finds at all satisfying is to enjoy life while you can. Since life is fleeting, troubles abound, and one day death will come, enjoy the simple pleasures of today:

This is what I have seen to be good: it is fitting to eat and drink and find enjoyment in all the toil with which one toils under the sun the few days of the life God gives us; for this is our lot. (Eccles. 5.18)

It is important to live life in the moment and to enjoy it as far as we can. As we heard in the previous chapter, some people find that their attempts to have a child, whether through fertility treatment or adoption, take too high a toll on their well-being and their relationships. They feel that they are destroying their ability to love others and to enjoy life through the painful struggle to have children. To them, the Teacher says: enjoy the gift of life while you can.

We turn now to the first chapter of the Bible, to the account of creation found in Genesis 1:

> Then God said, 'Let us make humankind in our image, according to our likeness; and let them have dominion over the fish of the sea, and over the birds of the air, and over the cattle, and over all the wild animals of the earth, and over every creeping thing that creeps upon the earth.'
>
> So God created humankind in his image,
> in the image of God he created them;
> male and female he created them.
>
> God blessed them, and God said to them, 'Be fruitful and multiply, and fill the earth and subdue it; and have dominion over the fish of the sea and over the birds of the air and over every living thing that moves upon the earth.' God said, 'See, I have given you every plant yielding seed that is upon the face of all the earth, and every tree with seed in its fruit; you shall have them for food. And to every beast of the earth, and to every bird of the air, and to everything that creeps on the earth, everything that has the breath of life, I have given every green plant for food.' And it was so. God saw everything that he had made, and indeed, it was very good. And there was evening and there was morning, the sixth day.
> (Gen. 1.26–31)

The first two chapters of Genesis absolutely teem with life. God speaks, and things come into being – sun, moon and stars appear; dry land is revealed and plants grow; the sea is filled with creatures; animals appear on land; finally, human beings are created. In C. S. Lewis's retelling of this story, when he describes the creation of Narnia by Aslan, the soil of the newly born world is so fertile that anything planted in it will grow. A broken bit of lamp post grows up into a new lamp post and a piece of toffee found in a child's pocket grows into a toffee tree (Lewis 1955, pp. 102, 140, 143). Some people seem to enjoy comparable fertility, conceiving multiple children with apparent ease. Some even have twins – a formidable achievement in the eyes of a person struggling with childlessness.

God says, 'Be fruitful and multiply'. God commands humankind to reproduce, and some of us cannot obey. More than that – God speaks God's creative word over us, but we prove to be barren soil. We are made in the image of God, filled with creative potential by our creator, and some of us cannot fulfil that potential. And that failure in one realm of human creativity and possibility can spill over into all areas of our lives. Serene Jones expresses this well:

> Women have told me that along with their inability to make a child comes a sense of their inability to make a future. When this happens, time stretches before them as a story of parching barrenness or violent bloodiness; in either case, it no longer stretches before them as a book that they are invited to write. (Jones 2009, p. 137)

I have a vivid memory of talking with some dear friends I have known for many years about my own deep sense of hopelessness. I was considering applying for a new job and my husband and I were beginning to explore adoption. They were listening kindly but they were puzzled by my profound negativity (I am generally a very positive person). I remember saying something highly illogical along these lines: 'I can't have a baby, I've been disappointed so many times. Why would adoption be any different?' Rationally, this makes no sense. There is no reason why a low ovarian reserve would impair my job prospects or make an adoption agency turn me down. But the sense of barrenness crept into almost every area of my life, such that I doubted my ability to achieve or to create anything at all. It was hard to feel any sense of positivity about the future.

As well as compounding the sadness of people whose bodies

cannot 'be fruitful and multiply', the Genesis account of creation may be seen as setting up a pattern of life into which some people simply do not fit. Male and female are apparently created to be together and to be fruitful, filling the earth with their children. People who have not found a life partner, who are in a same-sex couple, or who are unable to have children with their partner, may wonder where they fit – and the society around them will certainly remind them of their strangeness. In a video conversation created for World Childless Week, healthcare chaplain and pastor Sikhumbuzo Dube speaks movingly of the shame of childlessness in his home country of Zimbabwe. He describes a tradition of burying childless people with a rat tied to their back to express society's displeasure at their failure to do their duty and procreate.[4] There is a cruel sort of logic here, as children are necessary for society to function. Without the next generation, there will not be enough people to do the work or to look after elderly relatives; there will be no one to inherit the family name and property; ultimately the human race will die out. In the global north, Jody Day has written powerfully of the cruel stereotypes applied to women without children, particularly single women – 'dried up', 'spinster', 'crazy cat lady' (Day 2016, pp. 146f.). She writes from the UK context, but includes stories from women in the USA, Canada, Australia, Japan and Scandinavia. Day argues that, rather than being an economic necessity, in the wealthy global north motherhood is held up as the only way for women to achieve a meaningful life. According to this ideology, physical barrenness really does mean a barren life, as childless women are cut off from the most meaningful role it is possible to have. In her book, *Living the Life Unexpected: How to Find Hope, Meaning and a Fulfilling Future without Children*, Day spends considerable time debunking this myth in ways that are extremely helpful. She suggests that single childless women pose a threat to the patriarchy as they are neither 'someone's wife' nor 'someone's mother' (Day 2016, pp. 68f.). There is a considerable weight of pronatalist ideology to contend with – for men as well as women.

Jody Day's book *Living the Life Unexpected* is essentially a workbook for childless women to use to re-create their lives. While her work specifically focuses on childlessness in women, many of the principles do, I think, apply to all people struggling with childlessness. Day does not deny the depth of grief that childlessness can bring: indeed, she writes at length about the 'grief work' that needs to be done before a person can move on with their life. She argues, however, that childless women need not be 'stuck' in grief: that they can design a 'Plan B' which can be just as satisfying, meaningful, and filled with love. Day offers a number of helpful exercises to help women connect with the 'joy, movement and playfulness' that they may have lost in the sadness of their involuntary childlessness (Day 2016, p. 257). I suspect the principle of re-creating a life after heartbreak could helpfully be applied to all people. It may be hard to be creative when deep in the depression of grief; it may be impossible at that time to consider that the future might hold hope. And yet perhaps, once we have worked through the profound sadness of our inability to be fruitful in reproduction, we might claim our creative potential and give birth to new things.

To say this is not to put pressure on childless people to make their lives extraordinary because they could not be parents. Day jokingly refers to this as the 'Mother Teresa Complex', confessing that she briefly considered selling all her possessions and going to work with orphans in Laos:

> However, looking back on it now, I can see that parcelled up in that plan was a mixture of romanticized tragic glamour, an escape from the reality of my pain and a desire to have my loss witnessed and understood by others through heroic sacrifice: part of what I now term the 'Mother Teresa Complex.' I didn't think much about the orphans at all and it certainly wasn't about following my bliss; it was about following my pain. (Day 2016, pp. 277–8)

Day argues that the pressure to make your life 'mean something' because you don't have children is driven by misplaced shame. She urges her readers to question the narrative that parenthood is the most meaningful thing you can do, and asks why parents should not also be allowed to have big dreams for their lives (Day 2016, p. 287).

John McKeown has identified 'be fruitful and multiply' as the text most commonly cited by contemporary American pro-natalists, though he favours the term 'natalists' (McKeown 2014, p. 39). This school of thought argues that 'be fruitful and multiply' is a divine command that is still binding upon Christians who, they argue, should have large families – typically six or more children. McKeown cites various interpreters, however, from the early church fathers to Karl Barth, who understand this Old Testament command to be radically reinterpreted in the New Testament (McKeown 2014, pp. 52f.). Some pronatalists argue that creativity is part of what it means to carry the image of God. McKeown points out, however, that Jesus Christ presents us with a new image of God – a single person (McKeown 2014, p. 71). Furthermore, reproduction in the New Testament is understood in terms of preaching the gospel, and spiritual family takes precedence over biology. He quotes the third-century biblical scholar Eusebius at some length:

> He admits that reproduction was how God's people grew in the old covenant era, but now celibate 'preachers of the word … bring up not one or two children but a prodigious number' by spiritual birth … 'Increase and multiply and replenish the earth' … is 'fulfilled more truly and divinely' through evangelism and teaching (McKeown 2014, p. 60).

In the modern era, Karl Barth sees humans 'reflecting true parent-hood insofar as they teach the gospel' – this is the essence of Christian reproduction (McKeown 2014, p. 60). In 1 Timothy 1.2 and Titus 1.4, we see the apostle Paul addressing each of these men as his 'true son' in the faith; to the church at Corinth he declares: 'in Christ Jesus I became your father through the gospel' (1 Cor. 4.15). To childless people of faith, this is an incredibly powerful statement. We are no longer excluded from God's purposes or God's blessing by our childlessness. Biological lineage is no longer important. True family is now defined by those who follow Christ. Our inability to produce biological children is irrelevant in this new dispensation.

The Genesis account of creation may be painful to read when a childless person is in the depth of grief and coming to terms with their inability to conceive and nurture life. It may be hard to read when they are dealing with the weight of their society's expectations, unable to fulfil them by having children. As they begin to heal and to embrace the possibility of hope, however, they can perhaps re-read Genesis 1 with the attitude of the apostle Paul, and affirm that they too can be fruitful. The fruit of their lives may be different from the fruit of others, but their lives can also bring forth new life. Indeed, theologians such as Karl Barth would argue that the act of reproduction of most profound significance is still very much open to them. They can share the good news of God's love with others – a love that watched over them while they were still in the womb, and that watches over them still with unconditional positive regard. They can tell of this self-sacrificing love, poured out on the cross of Christ, in which he shared in all the shame and brokenness of humanity. They can speak of the empty tomb which proclaims Christ's victory over sin and death; which declares that God can and will raise even their childlessness. They can speak as people who have stared into the abyss: who have perhaps at times declared, 'everything is barren', and yet still know themselves to be held, loved and accepted by some-thing – someone – greater than themselves. People who have struggled with childlessness have a story to tell, and there is a world out there that needs their story. There are many millions of people living lives of 'quiet desperation', who need to know that God loves them and longs for them to receive that love.[5] In the global north, people may well be suspicious of organized religion, but fascinated by spirituality, and longing for authen-ticity. They do not need cheerful sanitized faith stories where everything always turns out fine. They need to know that, in the midst of terrible pain and utter brokenness, there is some-one who cares and in whom they can place their hope.

Creativity and possibility are not over once the prospect of having a baby is gone. Childless people may claim their creative nature and allow new things to grow in the soil of a life that has not brought forth children. We can claim God's creative word and give birth to other things. 'Be fruitful and multiply' need not be limited to the production of offspring. One of Madelyn Cain's respondents expresses beautifully the many creative possibilities open to human beings, regardless of their reproductive health: 'we give birth to ideas, to relationships, to works of art, to hope, to peace, to children, and to each other' (Cain 2001, p. 148).

We give birth to many things. To art, literature, craft. To gardens. To friendships and networks and community. To books and projects. To diplomas and degrees. To careers. To businesses, charities and social enterprises. To adoptive and foster families. And, the apostle Paul would add, to children of God. While the first Adam had a duty to reproduce and fill the earth, the last Adam was a single man who said, pointing to his disciples, 'Here are my mother and my brothers!' (Matt. 12.49).

The practice

Part of this chapter was written during the UK lockdown in spring 2020 which happened in response to the coronavirus pandemic. One of the common reactions to lockdown that I observed was the impulse to be creative. It started out with pictures of rainbows, often painted by children, being displayed in people's windows. Neighbours' children who were being homeschooled drew on the pavements with chalk. The shops all sold out of flour – doubtless partly because, initially at least, supplies of bread were unpredictable. Many people, however, faced with lots of time at home, experimented with baking bread and cakes. I tried some guerrilla gardening by mowing a labyrinth into some council-owned land next to my house.

Then we noticed that some streets had started hanging bunting. It was suggested in our road's WhatsApp group that we make bunting ourselves out of leftover fabric. Some people in the street had sewing machines; some had bored children to entertain; some had old bedding and other scrap fabric. One neighbour took photos of the technique for cutting bunting and posted it for others to see. Others left fabric on the doorsteps of those more confident of their sewing abilities. Then people got out their ladders and helped each other to hang the bunting along – and sometimes, in violation of the town council's instructions, across – the road. A couple of weeks later, other streets in the town hung bunting to celebrate the 75th anniversary of VE Day. On our street, it seemed to me simply a creative response to fear and boredom. A piece of benign vandalism bringing simple joy in the face of global fear. Pain and loss brought forth creativity.

One of the ways in which we can care for friends and family struggling with childlessness might be to notice and point out the ways in which we see them exercising their God-given creativity. Each person is different, and we all express creativity differently. Some of us are able to be creative at work: building things; initiating projects; bringing new ideas, techniques, products or businesses into being. Others perhaps exercise their creativity mainly in their spare time: creating beautiful or useful objects; making music, writing, painting; building community and seeking to improve the part of the world where they live. In the depths of grief, it may be hard to be creative, and it may be that nothing brings much joy. But part of the process of healing may be to realize gradually our creative potential and to develop more and more satisfaction in the things we create.

Katy started her blog, *Chasing Creation*, with the aim of 'designing an unexpectedly childfree life'. Her writing takes inspiration from Jody Day's work: she describes *Living the Life Unexpected* as 'the bible for those who are designing an unexpectedly childfree life'. Katy writes:

> I don't want to be defined by what I lack. For me, having a childfree mindset is aspirational. I know women who couldn't have kids but have created such beautiful lives that they would no longer trade them for parenthood. I don't know if I'm quite there yet but I know I'm getting closer each month. I love my current life and am enjoying the unique benefits that a life without children offers.

I wish I could tell my younger self that there is nothing here to pity. That womanhood does not equal motherhood. I wish I could tell her not to worry. That her life won't look how she expected, but it will be full of joy, meaning, love, and fulfillment.[6]

Katy tried for four years to conceive, finally coming to the realization that this was taking too high a physical and emotional toll. She had a hysterectomy, which greatly improved her quality of life, and began a journey of discovering how she might embrace her creative nature though childfree. In a post entitled, 'I'm not a mom, but I am a powerful source of creation', Katy makes a long list of the things she does create. She lists artistic pursuits, such as playing the ukulele, singing and writing music, DIY projects around the home, and photography. She lists the ways in which she creates a more just society by voting, by giving to good causes, through social activism, and in her work for a non-profit organization that seeks policy change on behalf of children. Katy enjoys growing vegetables, cooking healthy meals, and caring for the planet. She creates a supportive space for connection and awareness of endometriosis and infertility through her blog and social media accounts. She creates courage by letting go of fear; peace by practising forgiveness; knowledge through reading; meaning by identifying her dreams and following them. She intentionally creates a happy life.[7] For Katy, recovering from her four years of infertility and the sadness of not being able to have children is a creative pursuit. She explicitly specifies that she is creating her life and that she sees that life as bursting with creativity. Like the first two chapters of Genesis, like the fertile soil of Narnia, Katy's days, weeks and months teem with life.

This is an attitude that takes time to cultivate, and Katy herself acknowledges that she is 'not there yet'. Caring friends and family, seeing their loved one struggling with childlessness, may wish to comfort them by pointing out the many ways in which their life can still bring forth life. There is a delicate balance, however, between affirming a person's creative possibility and exhorting them to 'look on the bright side'. Jody Day offers helpful exercises throughout her book, which aim to help women work through their grief and begin to re-create their lives. She repeatedly acknowledges, however, that beginning to be creative may be very difficult and even frightening at first. People need to have been allowed to grieve before they can begin to embrace their creative potential (Day 2016, p. 282). It may be wisest for friends and pastoral carers to wait for the small green shoots of creative possibility to emerge, pointing them out when they see them. Rather than encouraging the person to take up a hobby they have always wanted to try, better to notice, appreciate and affirm the small creative acts that are the beginnings of healing and moving on. Rather than encouraging the person to get involved in the church, wait and see what interests them and encourage them to develop their ministry. Let re-creation happen at their pace, and rejoice with them as it does.

Notes

1 Winston 2015, chapter 5. Winston explains that even in 'natural' conception, most embryos are lost before the woman's period is due.

2 Of course, someone who does not want to have children may not experience infertility as a limitation. I have every respect for the decision some make to remain voluntarily childless. I am concerned in this book, however, with the experience of those who wish for children and find themselves unable to bear them.

3 Ellis 2003, p. 12, and 2006, p. 5. A friend has suggested to me that Anna the prophetess, described in Luke 2.36–38, could be one exception. She was widowed after seven years of marriage and then came to live in the temple. It seems likely that she bore no children.

4 Sikhumbuzo Dube, Robin Hadley, Andy Harrod and Michael Hughes, 2020, '4 guys from 3 continents', *World Childlessness Week*, 17 September, https://worldchildlessweek.net/thurs-17-2020/4-guys-from-3-continents. Dube is part of a community for men experiencing childlessness called The Clan of Brothers, accessed 7.3.2021.

5 This term was coined by Henry David Thoreau.

6 Katy, 2019, 'Childfree after infertility', *Chasing Creation*, 13 October, https://chasingcreation.org/childfree-after-infertility/, accessed 7.3.2021.

7 Katy, 2019, 'I'm not a mom, but I am a powerful source of creation', *Chasing Creation*, 18 August, https://chasingcreation.org/what-i-create/, accessed 7.3.2021.

5

Guilty

I never wanted to have IVF. I would have done almost anything to avoid it. Once my husband and I realized that we were unlikely to conceive without help, I wanted to go straight on to exploring adoption. I would love to say that it was because I am an altruistic person, but it was fear of IVF, rather than the desire to adopt, that was driving me at that time. The fear was twofold. First, it was fear of the physical demands of the treatment and its invasive nature that frightened me. Second, it was fear of the ethical dilemmas surrounding IVF that were bothering me. A third aspect that I had not grasped prior to treatment was the emotional toll that two cycles of IVF would take. I can still be taken by surprise, when writing or speaking about IVF, by a memory that comes back so fresh and so painful, more than three years after finishing treatment.

The ethical issues around IVF were, for me, both troubling and confusing. Almost no one could give me a straight answer. A person or couple undergoing IVF have to make certain ethical choices even before treatment can begin. Furthermore, although the female partner is considered 'the patient' in IVF, if she is trying to conceive with a male partner then both partners will need to agree on these choices. For example, if the female partner's own eggs are of poor quality, donated eggs can be used. If her partner's sperm is of poor quality, donated sperm can also be used. Thus, people undergoing IVF can effectively 'adopt' some or all of their child's genetic material, having a birth child who is not biologically theirs, or who does not have a biological link to their partner. It is well known that the quality of a woman's eggs deteriorates with age, and there is much individual variation, with no rhyme or reason. Two women of the same age may have eggs of very different quality, and this cannot be determined without a blood test. To complicate the decision still further, 'poor quality' eggs used in IVF can result in the birth of a healthy child – it is a game of probabilities rather than certainties. Once a woman has been referred for IVF, she may discover that she is considered unlikely to conceive a child using her own eggs, and she will have to make the difficult decision as to what to do next. Should she try IVF with her own eggs, which may give her smaller odds of success? Or should she get her name on a long waiting list for an egg donor, with the hope that the gift of someone else's better-quality eggs may allow her to conceive the child for which she longs? Likewise, the male partner may discover that his sperm quality makes fathering a child less likely. Sperm quality is something over which most men have very little control, although in some cases general health can be a factor: diet, exercise, recreational drug use and so on. There is some evidence that certain vitamin supplements improve sperm quality, but it is not an exact science. Furthermore, in some rare cases a man can be born with no sperm in his semen, a condition called azoospermia. It may be that donor sperm offers an individual or couple a better chance of conceiving through IVF. Same-sex couples and individuals contemplating IVF will not, of course, have any choice in the matter – they will need donated eggs or sperm in order to fulfil their dream of a child. UK law now states that children born using donor eggs or sperm have the right to trace and to contact their biological parent once they turn 18.[1] This introduces another element into the dilemma: the possibility that, at some point in the future, the donor will not remain a stranger, but may become part of the child's life.

Whether or not the person undergoing IVF is able to use their own eggs and partner's sperm, they will need to decide what should be done with any embryos that are created in treatment and not used within that cycle. IVF works by stimulating the ovaries to produce more than the one or two usually produced during the monthly cycle – ideally, 10–14 eggs. These eggs are then mixed with sperm and it is hoped that some will fertilize. Then, fertilized eggs are carefully kept and observed to see how they develop. Not all eggs fertilize, and not all fertilized eggs develop. There is much natural loss in IVF, hence the reason for the number of eggs collected. If the sperm fertilize one or more of the eggs and the result-ing embryos appear to be developing well, one or two of the 'best-quality'[2] embryos are transferred to the woman's uterus, and the rest are frozen. As multiple pregnancies involve a higher risk, generally just one embryo is transferred at a time. If the embryo fails to implant – and more often than not, they don't implant – the woman is given at least three months' rest for her body to recover before another embryo transfer is attempted. In the meantime, some embryos may not survive the freezing process – yet more loss.

In the happy event that the woman becomes pregnant and gives birth to a child, the rest of the embryos remain frozen until such a time as she may decide to try for another child. Once she has had all the children she wants to have, or has decided that the time is right to stop trying, there may be frozen embryos left over. These can be destroyed, donated for research, or donated to other couples or individuals who may not have eggs and sperm of sufficient quality for IVF to stand a reasonable chance of success. This means that there is a possibility that there may be children born that are biologically theirs, but raised by someone else.

For people of faith seeking to make ethical choices in treat-ment, it is very difficult to know what to do and where to turn. My husband and I are both committed Christians, and yet had different views of the ethics involved: we each drew the line at a different point. There are very clear guidelines for Roman Catholic Christians, for whom most fertility treatment is not permitted. Non-Catholics contemplating fertility treatment will struggle to find any concrete information to help them make these decisions, however. As we approached the hospital appointment at which we would be referred for IVF (unless a miracle happened in the meantime), I became more and more worried. It did not look as if my reprieve would come and I was confused as to the right way forward. I was desperate to get pregnant, but terrified of making a decision that was unethical. I was terrified of angering God. I was terrified of having to live with a decision that I later regretted.

We were in the fortunate position of not needing donor eggs or sperm, and so did not have the dilemma of whether or not to adopt a stranger's genetic material. We did, however, have to consider what we would do with our embryos before they had even been created. I had read about a Christian couple who had chosen to have fewer eggs collected precisely because they did not want to have the dilemma of potentially having to destroy embryos that were not needed. The husband expresses his concerns eloquently:

> The doctor says it's just a blob of tissue. The Christian doctors I ask avoid answering directly. 'You're over-analyzing it,' someone at church said. 'My friend got a beautiful baby girl through IVF. Just do it.' Before God, I can't use this technology if it destroys life. Yet no one will help me decide if it does or doesn't. Those ignorant of the procedure just want us to be happy, and those who know stay noncommittal. God isn't saying a word either way. (Voysey 2013, p. 10)

As we sat in the fertility clinic talking to our consultant, discussing our treatment and signing forms, I explained this dilemma to him. He replied that the only way of collecting fewer eggs would be to put me on a lower dose of hormones, so that my ovaries would be stimulated less and would produce fewer follicles. He then said something that I have always remembered, and that was one of the few really helpful things I was told when considering treatment. 'I am a Muslim,' he explained. 'I believe that life begins when the heart starts beating. That is between five and six weeks of development.' Embryos used in IVF treatment never, by law, pass two weeks of development (Warnock 2002, p. 35), and are usually either used or frozen once they are five days old. For non-Catholics considering fertility treatment, it is very hard to find any helpful fixed point around which to make ethical decisions. To hear a person of faith explaining his view so clearly was enormously comforting to me.

One of the things I learned during fertility treatment was the unpredictable nature of the process. I went into IVF worried about creating life only to destroy it; as it turned out, this was not a problem. I responded so poorly to the medication that the doctors struggled to get any eggs out of me, even when I was eventually put on the highest dose of medication. A booklet published by the Christian Medical Fellowship recommends that Christians opt for egg freezing rather than embryo freezing – in other words, that as many eggs as possible are collected, but fewer eggs mixed with sperm to produce embryos (Roach and Taylor 2014, p. 28). This is because, in the view of Roach and Taylor, eggs do not have the same moral significance as embryos, and hence fewer embryos are risked in freezing and thawing. Doubtless this could be a possible option for some individuals and couples, although my own experiences revealed to me the wisdom of trying to collect and fertilize as many eggs as possible in a typical round of IVF. As embryos are lost at every stage, and this cannot be known in advance, using fewer eggs risks ending up with few or no usable embryos.

There were moments when the anxiety induced by the ethical decisions we were being forced to make became overwhelming for me. One of these moments came just a few weeks before our first cycle of IVF, when I was still deeply ambivalent about the process. A friend told me about a prayer ministry run by her church and suggested that I make an appointment. I liked the idea of being prayed for by people who did not know me, and did not know that I was a Christian minister. I drove to a church a few miles away and was prayed for by two women in their sixties whose calm intercessions were very soothing. They suggested that, in my mind, I ask Jesus for what I wanted. I pictured myself begging with tears in my eyes for a child. They continued to pray and a sense of peace descended on me. As I got in my car to drive home afterwards, however, doubts arose in my mind. Maybe this was wrong. Maybe God was angry with me. Maybe God did not want me to have fertility treatment, and was challenging me to stop. As I drove home, the fear stayed with me. I went to bed and slept well, but woke up in the morning still fearful. Unwisely, I picked up my tablet and started googling 'ethics in fertility treatment'. It felt as if the fear was literally rising in my throat. I have suffered with anxiety on and off since I was a teenager, and the ethical dilemmas presented by fertility treatment played havoc with this pre-existing disposition towards fear and self-doubt.

Fortunately, on that day, two things happened. First, a thought came to my mind which set me free. It occurred to me that, while God does speak to challenge and correct us at times, God does not seek to frighten us. God does not terrify and shame us into obedience. If God had wanted to steer me away from the treatment, God would have spoken in a way that brought peace rather than fear. Suddenly it became very clear: whatever it was that was telling me I was being selfish and sinful in seeking fertility treatment was not God.

Second, I had a visit from a friend and mentor who – in the wonderful providence of God – had been a fertility nurse before retraining for Christian ministry. She was assigned to me as a mentor when I left theological college, newly married and, at that time, blissfully unaware of my fertility problems. It seemed that God had put in my life the very person who was best placed to help me in my fear and confusion. Her view, as an evangelical Christian with medical training, was that IVF simply re-created outside the body processes that usually occurred within it, unseen. Even women enjoying good reproductive health lose many embryos created by natural conception, as they fail to implant and are lost before the woman is aware she is pregnant. IVF re-created in a test tube what should have been happening inside my body. I needed to see my fear of creating embryos that would not survive in the context of the many embryos that other women lost all the time without knowing it. Early embryo loss was, in an important sense, a natural process.

I have recounted my own experiences in order to try to frame the ethical issues facing people struggling with childlessness. I cannot provide – indeed, no one can provide – a theologically correct answer that will satisfy everyone. I am simply attempting to set out the various aspects of the dilemma for the benefit of people who are seeking to make decisions in treatment, as well as those supporting them. When my husband and I were seeking treatment, we made decisions that we felt were right – and in some cases we disagreed, where one of us felt an action was acceptable and the other was unsure. I do not believe that I have the right to tell anyone what they should do. Doubtless this is partly down to personality: I am not the kind of person who generally feels comfortable telling others what to do. It is partly theological: I am a Baptist minister, and Baptists believe in freedom of conscience and resist fixed statements of faith. Partly it is a question of hermeneutics: I love the Bible, and I know that it does not have any clear answers for us on this issue. The Bible says nothing of the status of a human embryo. And partly it is pastoral: because I have been there, and I know how incredibly painful it can be to make these decisions. The stakes are so high, emotions are fraught, and this is not a state in which it is easy to make important decisions.

The consolation

Having considered the difficult dilemmas faced by people who undergo fertility treatment, we now turn to the Bible and to Christian theological resources for help. I do not have the space here – or, frankly, the training – to attempt a thorough examination of the ethical issues, but I will offer a brief overview, drawing from three different streams of Christian theology. This may provide some consolation by, at the very least, offering some potential ways forward for decision-making. It would have helped me greatly to have had more resources to help me consider the issues in the light of Scripture and theology and come to my own conclusions. Finally, we will consider some biblical texts for wisdom and consolation.

The Roman Catholic Church has very clear guidelines for individuals and couples considering fertility treatment. For the most part, it is not permitted. The catechism of the Catholic Church acknowledges and affirms the pain of infertility, and welcomes research into fertility, as children are received as an unequivocal good. Treatments that separate sex from procreation are, however, 'morally unacceptable'. IVF separates the sexual act from the act of conception. The male partner masturbates into a small plastic cup; the woman has her eggs removed using a needle, under sedation. The eggs and sperm are mixed in the laboratory and conception happens outside the body. IVF is not permitted for Catholics.[3]

Furthermore, treatments that introduce a third person in order to conceive the longed-for child, such as sperm or egg donation and surrogacy, are 'gravely immoral'. They 'infringe the child's right to be born of a father and mother known to him and bound to each other by marriage. They betray the spouses' "right to become a father and a mother only through each other."'[4] The catechism also makes reference to *Donum Vitae*, the Congregation for the Doctrine of the Faith's *Instruction on Respect for Human Life in its Origin and on the Dignity of Procreation*, published on 22 February 1987. This instruction considers issues around fertility treatment in detail. In the introduction we read that life begins at the moment of conception, at which point the immortal soul is created, and 'God alone is the Lord of life from its beginning until its end: no one can, in any circumstance, claim for himself the right to destroy directly an innocent human being.'[5] It is clear that the destruction of unwanted embryos after fertility treatment has ended is not permitted for Catholics. Not only that:

> *The freezing of embryos*, even when carried out in order to preserve the life of an embryo – cryopreservation – *constitutes an offence against the respect due to human beings* by exposing them to grave risks of death or harm to their physical integrity and depriving them, at least temporarily, of maternal shelter and gestation, thus placing them in a situation in which further offences and manipulation are possible.[6]

IVF is deeply problematic for Roman Catholics, then: first, because it separates sex from procreation; second, because it involves the freezing of embryos and consequent risk; and third, because it can involve the destruction of unwanted embryos. Furthermore, sperm and egg donation and surrogacy are beyond the pale, because it is only seen as appropriate for a child to be born of a heterosexual married couple.

In a booklet published by the Christian Medical Fellowship (CMF), Roach and Taylor express similar concerns, albeit from a very different theological perspective. They conclude, however, that IVF is acceptable for Christians, within certain parameters. CMF has an evangelical statement of faith and describes itself as an organization that 'unites and equips Christian doctors and nurses to live and speak for Jesus Christ'. According to its website, around 5,000 doctors, 900 medical and nursing students, and 300 nurses and midwives, are currently members.[7] Roach and Taylor argue that, for Christians contemplating IVF treatment, the production of spare embryos is the key ethical dilemma. They echo the Catholic Church's concern about the freezing of embryos, citing the survival rate of approximately two-thirds of embryos, following freezing and thawing, as problematic. They liken the freezing of embryos to taking three children on a journey to a foreign country, knowing only two will survive the journey (Roach and Taylor 2014, pp. 19–21). This seems to me to be an inappropriately sentimental and misleading characterization of the dilemma involved. When we were discussing our fertility treatment in 2017 we were told by our consultant that embryo survival rates were closer to 80–85 per cent. Nevertheless, there is a significant risk that has to be acknowledged. Along with the Roman Catholic Church, Roach and Taylor also express concerns about the need for masturbation in fertility treatment, and about the use of donor eggs and sperm. They resolve the masturbation issue by recommending that the husband focus on fantasizing about his wife, but argue that Christians should not, in their view, accept donor eggs or sperm, or consider surrogacy. Like the Roman Catholic Church, they are concerned with the notion of involving a third person in the marriage (Roach and Taylor 2014, pp. 23–5). Single and gay Christians seeking fertility treatment are not considered at all.

Roach and Taylor have some practical suggestions for avoiding the risks associated with embryo freezing. They suggest that all embryos be transferred to the woman's uterus in the cycle in which they are created. They also recommend egg freezing rather than embryo freezing (Roach and Taylor 2014, p. 28). These suggestions do mitigate some of the risks but, unfortunately, not all. There are also practical problems. For example, there is no way of knowing how many eggs will fertilize and develop into viable embryos. Assuming that ovarian stimulation and egg retrieval are successful, let us imagine that ten eggs are collected, and all are mixed with sperm. On average, around 60 per cent will fertilize,[8] resulting in six embryos. They may not all be viable but it would not be unreasonable to expect three or four embryos that look viable, and suitable for embryo transfer after three days. Single embryo transfer is now recommended, however, due to the risk of multiple births. Going into fertility treatment, I was naively excited by the possibility of becoming pregnant with twins. But a twin pregnancy carries a significant risk, both to the mother and to the unborn babies. The risks of miscarriage, stillbirth and foetal abnormality are higher. Most IVF clinics will only transfer one or possibly two embryos. To transfer four would be irresponsible. Robert Winston explains that Human Fertilisation and Embryology Authority regulations stipulate that generally only one embryo should be transferred, with exceptions made for older women or those who have already had failed treatment (Winston 2015, chapter 5). To transfer three or four embryos would be to chance a higher-risk pregnancy. Instead of losing a three-day-old embryo in freezing and thawing, you would be risking miscarrying a foetus or losing a baby or babies through stillbirth.

An alternative would be to freeze half the eggs that are collected – say, five out of ten eggs – and to mix the others with sperm. Assuming a 60 per cent fertilization rate, just three eggs would be fertilized, and they may not all develop normally. Using a smaller number of eggs in treatment increases the risk of having no viable embryo to transfer, and thus the likelihood of needing further cycles to produce further embryos in order to achieve a successful embryo transfer. The complexities of the treatment mean that it is not necessarily possible to make all our ethical decisions at the beginning: individuals and couples have to be prepared to adapt as they discover how the woman's body responds to ovarian stimulation and how easy it proves to achieve a viable embryo once eggs and sperm are mixed.

In a section relating to its stance on abortion and contraception, the website for the Methodist Church in Britain adopts a view of the status of the embryo that is more nuanced. References are made to a 1976 Methodist Conference statement on the embryo's right to life:

> There is never any moment from conception onwards when the fetus totally lacks human significance ... However the degree of this significance manifestly increases.
>
> ... The result of the coming together of human sperm and ovum is obviously human. The appearance of the 'primitive streak' (the beginning of the neurological system) after some fourteen days is an important stage. However for many weeks after this event, natural abortion[9] will continue to bring about the termination of over 50% of embryos.
>
> Fertilisation, implantation and subsequent development are parts of a continuous process. It is simply not possible to identify the single moment when a new human person begins. The right of the embryo to full respect clearly increases throughout a pregnancy.[10]

Like the Roman Catholic Church, and the evangelical Christian doctors who write for CMF, the Methodist Church is concerned with the protection of the embryo. The Methodist view does not seem to insist, however, that an embryo has the same moral significance as a human baby. In 2008 the Methodist Conference received the report *Created in God's Image: An Ecumenical Report on Contemporary Challenges and Principles Relating to Early Human Life*.[11] The report includes a helpful summary of different views of the status of an embryo. The 'absolute' view holds that an embryo is fully human from the moment of conception and should be given the same protections and dignity given to a child after birth. The 'gradualist' view holds that, while the embryo is human from the moment of conception, its moral and theological significance increases with time. Both of these positions are held by practising Christians.[12]

The position of the Roman Catholic Church, as well as that taken by the conservative evangelical CMF publication, would seem to represent an absolute view. Hence the freezing and thawing of embryos, which constitutes a risk, can legitimately be compared with taking three children on a long journey, which only two are likely to survive. A gradualist position would acknowledge the human status of embryos while perhaps making allowance for the risks involved in fertility treatment. In a section discussing the treatment of 'spare' embryos:

> What is right will depend on what we consider to be the appropriate level of care for the embryo at this stage in its development. Opinions will range from those for whom disposal and research are unlikely to be acceptable options to those who might find no intrinsic difficulty with careful disposal at a point before differentiation has occurred.[13]

'Differentiation' here refers to the point at which the cells of the embryo begin to differentiate and the central nervous system starts to form, which occurs after 14 days. Before this point, some cells will become part of the placenta, and not part of the human body. UK law makes a distinction between an embryo before and after 14 days of development and it is illegal to keep and to conduct research on an embryo of 14 days and above (Warnock 2002, pp. 35–6). Thus UK law offers certain boundaries within which fertility treatment and research must take place.

The report goes on to outline three ways of approaching ethical decisions. First, consequentialist theories, of which utilitarianism is the best known. Utilitarianism maintains that the ethical choice is that which achieves the greatest good for the greatest number. Second, deontological theories require obedience to a set of rules which can be universalized. A deontological approach states that we should not do something unless we think everyone should do it. Finally, virtue ethics takes a different approach. Virtue theory asks, not 'what should I do?' but 'what sort of person should I be?'[14] The Bible contains rules to follow, but the biblical writers knew nothing of the intricacies of fertility or of the technology we have available to us now. It is very difficult to apply biblical rules and principles to fertility treatment and, in doing so, Christians have come to different conclusions. Many Christian denominations simply do not have rules governing human decisions in fertility treatment.

A deontological approach might turn to the Ten Commandments for guidance. However, the Ten Commandments do not, unfortunately, help very much with the complexities of fertility treatment. Some Christians would doubtless argue that the sixth commandment, 'do not commit murder', and the seventh, 'do not commit adultery', should apply in the case of embryo destruction and of donor eggs and sperm. This is a valid, if harsh, interpretation, but other interpretations are possible. One could just as easily use Genesis 16 or 30.1–13 to argue for the validity of surrogacy, for example. In the Old Testament we find many examples where a third person aids the intimate process of producing children. In Chapter 1 we considered the case of the slave-girl Hagar, compelled to bear Abram's child when Sarai's body seems unable to do so. In Genesis 30 we read of Jacob's wife, Rachel, offering him her maidservant, Bilhah, 'that she may bear upon my knees and that I too may have children through her' (Gen. 30.3). Rachel's sister, Leah, the less loved, in the same way offers her maid, Zilpah, once she seems to have passed the age of childbearing. In this early form of surrogacy, a third person comes into the marriage in order that children may be conceived. While Sarai's use of Hagar does not have happy consequences, there does not seem to be any condemnation of Rachel and Leah or their maids, either overt or implied. Many Christians, certainly in Western Europe and America, would see such actions as unethical today. We might perhaps bear this in mind when we take a dim view of certain options in modern fertility treatment, which are clinical processes involving no sexual infidelity.

A utilitarian approach may be helpful in navigating these ethical dilemmas – figuring out what would bring about the greatest good for the greatest number. But how does one weigh up embryos within that calculation? If an individual or couple enjoy great happiness, along with their wider family, over the birth of a baby conceived through IVF, how much does it matter that three embryos are destroyed, or perish during freezing? This question is impossible to answer.

The Bible has a great deal to say about virtues, however, so this may be a more promising starting-point. When considering fertility treatment, we might consider the fruit of the Spirit:

> … the fruit of the Spirit is love, joy, peace, patience, kindness, generosity, faithfulness, gentleness, and self-control. There is no law against such things. (Gal. 5.22–23)

We might ask ourselves, for example, what is the loving thing to do? What actions would promote joy and make for peace? How might I act with patience? and so on. There is not, of course, a set of right responses to these questions. They will not generate for us the clear, black-and-white answers that we perhaps crave. They will not tell us which treatment options are acceptable and which ones are not. Perhaps, however, they might allow the Spirit to speak to us. Perhaps, rather than anxiously trying to determine the 'right' thing to do, we might ask ourselves what the fruit of God's Spirit might look like in the situation in which we find ourselves.

Love and joy are surely some of the chief motivators for the desire to have children. People wanting children want to bring into the world another person they can love and cherish. Most parents report that they love their children, and that they bring their parents joy. Not happiness, necessarily – some surveys have found that people report lower levels of satisfaction with life after having children[15] – but a deeper kind of gladness that transcends broken nights, endless mundane domestic tasks, bickering between siblings and troubled teenage years. I felt a strange kind of joy when I heard that my eggs had fertilized; when I looked at a telescopic image of our embryos; when I sat watching my embryo transfers on an ultrasound monitor. The embryo is pushed out of the test tube through a catheter into the uterus and, as it goes, it looks like a shooting star. There is the potential for much love and joy through fertility treatment. On the flipside, we may wonder what the loving way to treat an embryo might be. To bring it into being is to take the risk that it may perish, either accidentally through freezing and thawing, or through deliberate destruction. This is the risk all parents take, of course – the risk God took when God created other creatures. To live is to experience the risk of harm. To love is to experience the risk of loss. The greater context is the desire to bring forth a creature – a baby – to love and cherish. This risks the loss of embryos in the process.

What course of action will make for peace? What will bring that shalom for which we all long, for which God longs – peace with one another, peace in our communities, peace with our environment, peace between us and God? What will bring peace in our bodies? For some, perhaps, the pathway to peace will be through treatment that enables them to know that they have done everything they can to achieve a pregnancy – even if it does not work. For others, perhaps peace might mean giving their body a rest from the demands they are making of it. Not putting their body through the rigours of injections, hormones, blood tests, invasive examinations and surgery. Each person experiencing infertility will need to find the path of peace.

According to the Amplified Bible, patience is 'not the ability to wait, but how we act while waiting' (Gal. 5.22). Behaving well while waiting can, however, be a tall order. In Chapter 3 I explored the ways in which the delays of fertility investigations and treatment can put the most patient person to the test. Patience was the virtue least apparent in my life during the three and a half years I was trying to conceive. Being told to relax and be patient did not go down well with me during that time. I never felt that I was a very good role model of a person experiencing adversity. I did not exhibit the serenity or simple trust that I imagined a really faithful Christian would demonstrate. Patience is of course related to faith and trust, which we explored in Chapter 4. We can be patient in suffering when we have faith that we will be delivered. In Chapter 4 I suggested a number of things for which we might trust God as we endure the powerlessness of childlessness: for example, that God is with us; that God cares; that God can and will bring resurrection. I wonder whether, when we consider the ethics of fertility treatment, there might be another aspect to patience – the patience to make a decision well, out of careful reflection rather than anxious impulsiveness. Perhaps patience might mean taking plenty of time to consider what we should do before God.

Let us now consider the beautiful words of Psalm 139. The psalmist declares that God saw us while we were still in the womb:

> For it was you who formed my inward parts;
>   you knit me together in my mother's womb.
> I praise you, for I am fearfully and wonderfully made.
>   Wonderful are your works;
> that I know very well.
>   My frame was not hidden from you,
> when I was being made in secret,
>   intricately woven in the depths of the earth.
> Your eyes beheld my unformed substance.
> In your book were written
>   all the days that were formed for me,
>   when none of them as yet existed.
> (Ps. 139.13–16)

These words are particularly poignant for those of us who are struggling with childlessness. Does God see the unformed substance of our eggs and sperm? Is it God who knits our embryos together – perhaps initially in a laboratory rather than the womb? If God is involved in the process, right at the beginnings of life, what does that mean for those of us who are interfering with the 'natural' way of doing things? If God is involved in the creation of our embryos – if they are God's, rather than ours, fearfully and wonderfully made – then how do we make decisions that may involve destroying them, or losing them in the freezing and thawing process? If God is involved at this stage, what does God think about donor eggs and sperm – other people brought into this intimate process of creating life?

Years ago, when I was working as a teacher, a Christian youth worker came in to take a school assembly, and he read from Psalm 139. He explained to the students that they were known and loved by God: that God had cared about them since they were in the womb. One of my colleagues was suspicious. She clearly thought he was making a political point about abortion. Christians have, after all, a reputation for having strong views over what goes on in the womb. I had the advantage of knowing the Bible a little better than my agnostic friend, and I did not think that was what he was doing at all. I think he was simply assuring the young people that they were known, loved and cherished by God. Because this, after all, is the heart of this psalm. The verses about the womb jump out at those of us who are concerned with what goes on inside it, but their function is to illustrate the depth and all-pervasiveness of God's knowledge and God's love. When I was contemplating fertility treatment, frightened and miserable, I remember my mother saying to me: 'You don't have to do this.' She was concerned about the emotional toll it was taking on me, as I grappled with the ethical issues and became increasingly anxious about the demands of the treatment. I was deeply grateful to her for saying it, even though I did go ahead with the treatment in the end. Because what I heard beneath her words was this: you are just as precious as the baby for which you long. I wanted my own baby but, many years before, I had been her baby. I was beating myself up over the difficult decisions I was having to make, and she was telling me that I was important too. My well-being mattered. This, surely, is the heart of Psalm 139. It is not a prophetic text, standing up for the rights of the foetus. It is not a piece of Old Testament law. It is a worshipful reflection, a song that reminds us that God saw *us* when *we* were in the womb. That God loves us and will never leave us. That we are as precious as the babies for which we long:

> Where can I go from your spirit?
>   Or where can I flee from your presence?
> If I ascend to heaven, you are there;
>   if I make my bed in Sheol, you are there.

If I take the wings of the morning
    and settle at the farthest limits of the sea,
even there your hand shall lead me,
    and your right hand shall hold me fast.
If I say, 'Surely the darkness shall cover me,
    and the light around me become night',
even the darkness is not dark to you;
    the night is as bright as the day,
    for darkness is as light to you.
(Ps. 139.7–12)

The practice

I have already explained that I do not personally believe I have the right, as a friend or as a pastoral counsellor, to tell anyone what they should do. I do not believe that people struggling with childlessness need the kind of pastoral care that gives them a list detailing what is acceptable and what is not. Catholic priests will, of course, follow the direction of the Roman Catholic Church. I deeply respect the Catholic Church and its laws – in this section I am essentially speaking to church leaders in denominations that do not have firm rules regarding fertility treatment. Ministers, priests and pastoral carers will want to help Christians struggling with childlessness to understand how their faith might interact with their fertility treatment. They will need to discover how to help vulnerable people experiencing infertility to navigate the complex ethical decisions before them and to manage the emotional fallout.

The first helpful thing they can do is to become informed. To read about infertility, childlessness, miscarriage and still-birth. Reading this book will, I hope, give people who do not have any direct experience of childlessness an insight into the issues involved, so that they may better support those going through it. As I have already mentioned, I was exceptionally fortunate in having a mentor assigned to me as part of my work in the church who happened to have been a nurse in a fertility clinic before training as a minister. I had pastoral support from someone who understood the details of fertility treatment and who was able to speak wisdom when I was in a flat spin. Most carers will not need this level of knowledge, but there are plenty of books and websites that give an overview of the process. I would highly recommend Robert Winston's *The Essential Fertility Guide* as a very clear, very compassionate and down-to-earth guide to issues around infertility, diagnosis and treatment. I have already referred extensively to the excellent blog *Saltwater and Honey*, which was started by two clergy couples experiencing infertility. Lizzie and Dave Lowrie have suffered the agony of six miscarriages, with no medical explanation and no treatment offered that might help. Sheila and Elis Matthews could not conceive due to Elis's extremely rare condition called azoospermia, meaning that he was born with no sperm in his semen. The Matthews have had a child through sperm donation; the Lowries are childless. The blog is a treasure trove of honest storytelling, vulnerable questioning and practical suggestions, including helpful liturgies.[16]

Even more important, however, is simply to be there and to listen. Each individual or couple will have a unique experience of childlessness. Some may have a particular diagnosis to deal with; others will have been given no explanation – perhaps because it is not possible to find one. Some people cannot seem to achieve a pregnancy; others can get pregnant but suffer the devastation of recurrent miscarriage. Some will be in the fortunate position of receiving fertility treatment on the NHS; many will have to find the money for some or all of their treatment, and so on top of the ethical dilemmas they may be assessing the wisdom of borrowing money to enable their dream to happen. Each person or couple will have their own story to tell, and they need to be able to tell it, and for it to be held and heard. They do not need attempts to make them feel better that dismiss, minimize or explain away their pain. They certainly do not need to be lectured about faith in adversity or reassured that God is good and has a plan. They need their pain to be recognized and their struggle to be shared. They need a companion on the journey.

I have loosely structured each of the first five chapters of this book around the pastoral cycle of theological reflection. I wonder if this approach could be fruitful and helpful in offering pastoral care to people navigating dilemmas in fertility treatment. Perhaps, after the person or couple have been able to share their experience, a short passage of Scripture could be read and dwelt upon together. In this way, the carer might create a space that enables the Holy Spirit to speak into a situation that is painful, difficult and emotionally fraught. This requires a high degree of trust and vulnerability, and not all people experiencing childlessness will be comfortable with it. An alternative is to suggest passages that the person or couple might read and consider on their own, with the offer of a reflective conversation should they wish to have it later on. Psalm 139 is an obvious passage to offer – although it probably needs to be handled delicately. Other possibilities could include:

- 1 Corinthians 13.4–7 – A meditation on the nature of self-sacrificing love. What does love look like in this situation? What is the loving thing to do?
- Romans 12.1–2, 9–18 – A description of a life transformed in Christ.
- 1 Kings 19.1–13 – Elijah meets God at Horeb.

The precise passages that are offered probably matter less than the spirit in which they are offered, and the context of a loving pastoral relationship. God can speak in all kinds of ways through all kinds of media. What is needed is that people experiencing childlessness feel loved and heard and that they have companionship on the lonely road they are walking – a road that involves making difficult choices. They need to be reminded that they are making these choices before a God who loves them, and who will love them no matter what.

Notes

1 'Using donated eggs, sperm or embryos in treatment', *Human Fertilisation & Embryology Authority*, www.hfea.gov.uk/treatments/ explore-all-treatments/using-donated-eggs-sperm-or-embryos-in-treat ment/, accessed 17.1.2021.

2 Winston argues that it is actually impossible to tell the 'quality' of an embryo by looking at it through a microscope. Nevertheless, there are various criteria used to classify embryos and to make decisions in treatment.

3 The Catechism of the Catholic Church, III, 2, www.vatican.va/ archive/ccc_css/archive/catechism/p3s2c2a6.htm, §2373-77.

4 The Catechism of the Catholic Church, III, 2, §2373-77.

5 *Donum Vitae*, 22 February 1987, Congregation for the Doctrine of the Faith Instruction on Respect for Human Life in its Origin and on the Dignity of Procreation.

6 *Donum Vitae*, I, 6.

7 Christian Medical Fellowship, 'Beliefs, values and identity', *CMF*, www.cmf.org.uk/about/beliefs-values-and-identity/, accessed 17.1.2021.

8 See Winston 2015, chapter 10.

9 'Natural abortion' is an unfortunate phrase which simply refers to the natural loss of an embryo that is not viable.

10 'Abortion and contraception', *The Methodist Church*, www. methodist.org.uk/about-us/the-methodist-church/views-of-the-church/ abortion-and-contraception/, accessed 7.3.2021.

11 Working Group on Human Embryology and Early Human Life for the Methodist Church, 2008, *Created in God's Image: An Ecumenical Report on Contemporary Challenges and Principles Relating to Early Human Life*, available from www.methodist.org.uk/about-us/ the-methodist-conference/conference-reports/conference-reports-2008/, accessed 7.3.2021.

12 *Created in God's Image*, p. 3.

13 *Created in God's Image*, p. 14.

14 *Created in God's Image*, pp. 31–2.

15 See, for example, Cain 2001, p. 16.

16 www.saltwaterandhoney.org.

6

So, What Now?

I think that one of the things we must learn how to do is suffer together. We are glad for all the wonderful medications and ways to relieve suffering today, but there are moments when we must go through difficult times together.[1]

For a person struggling with childlessness, church can be both the best and the worst place to be. Churches can be communities where people going through pain experience love, belonging and care in profoundly healing ways. They can also – like any gathering of people – have patterns of thought and behaviour that damage people and make them feel like outsiders. The worst things that have been said to me about my childlessness have been said by Christians. At the same time, I have had conversations with Christians that have brought me great healing and I have experienced tender care and love given by the Church.

Research suggests that around 10–15 per cent of couples in the UK experience problems in conceiving at some point in their relationship.[2] Many of these couples will take longer than they hoped to conceive but will go on to do so eventually. There are likely to be people in most churches who have experienced infertility, or whose close family have experienced this struggle, although most people will not experience long-term infertility. With people marrying and starting families later in life than their parents and grandparents, however, the numbers of people experiencing both temporary and permanent infertility are likely to rise.

Childlessness is a minority experience, albeit probably a growing minority, and yet brokenness takes many forms. People sitting in church, or participating in church online, need help to make sense of their experiences – including their most difficult experiences – before God, and this is not restricted to people struggling with childlessness. There are so many ways in which life hurts people, and this hurt can mess up our relationship with God. I firmly believe that worship, preaching, pastoral care – all the ways in which we seek to help congregations make sense of their experiences before God – need to engage with the most painful realities and confusing questions of life. This kind of worship, preaching and pastoral care will make churches safe places, not just for people struggling with childlessness, but for all those who live with bitter disappointment and chronic pain.

In this chapter I offer some resources for ministers and other leaders in local churches. In section one I offer some advice for those pastorally caring for people struggling with childlessness. Section two includes some suggestions for public worship, particularly at sensitive points in the liturgical year. Section three is the longest, and includes commentary to assist preachers in including certain challenging texts in their preaching programmes, and applying them to people whose lives are marked by struggle. Finally, section four is a list of resources to which people struggling with childlessness can be signposted, and that will enrich the knowledge of people looking to support them.

Section one: Caring for people struggling with childlessness

Childlessness is just one of the many painful struggles people go through in this life, and all of the principles of good pastoral care still apply. Listening without judgement; showing empathy and concern; checking in regularly without imposing oneself; respecting confidentiality – these practices will go a long way towards helping people struggling with childlessness to feel loved, seen and heard. There are elements of the experience of childlessness that make it distinctive, however, and that have prompted me to offer a few pointers to those who care pastorally for them.

The most important thing for pastoral carers to understand is that involuntary childlessness causes real grief. This was explored at length in Chapter 2. It is a strange kind of grief, however, because it often has no particular focus: there is usually no body, no funeral, and no public acknowledgement of what has been lost. In the case of late miscarriage and stillbirth, the loss is treated as a death, the baby's remains are treated with dignity, and there is a funeral and a chance to say goodbye. Most pregnancy loss takes place much earlier, however, often before the pregnant woman has started to tell people beyond her immediate family and friends that she is expecting a child. Loss during fertility treatment happens earlier still. Eggs fail to fertilize; fertilized eggs fail to develop; transferred embryos fail to implant in the womb. And then there is a more abstract kind of loss: the loss of children who will never be. The loss of a future we hoped for that will never come to pass. I have never knowingly been pregnant and did not mourn specific embryos – although some people do see their embryos as children. And yet I felt very keenly the loss of a dream. The loss of a possibility. The loss of a gift most others receive so easily. It is a loss that can be hard for others to understand. While I was in the process of writing this book, people told me of miscarriages that were dismissed by others as insignificant. Sometimes people do not understand how someone can grieve for a person they have never known. Even Rabbi Harold Kushner, whose book *When Bad Things Happen to Good People* is extremely compassionate and wise, and helped me greatly, vastly underestimates the significance of pregnancy loss.[3] And yet this sense of loss is real, intensely painful, and must be acknowledged before healing can take place. A minister asked me once whether it was appropriate for them to support a woman going through childlessness, because they themselves had biological children. I reassured them that many of the people who helped me the most as I wrestled with my childlessness had biological children themselves. You do not need to have gone through the experience yourself to empathize. You just need to be willing to listen and to acknowledge the pain.

Another aspect of the experience of childlessness that makes it distinctive is the secrecy in which it is shrouded. Although childlessness is in some ways very public – everyone can see that you do not have children, and may wonder why – it is also intensely private (Ellis 2006, p. 6). People may be much slower to come to the minister or pastoral care coordinator to disclose their struggles with infertility and childlessness than with other medical issues. This is for all kinds of good reasons. Discussing infertility involves discussing sex and genitalia – not a subject for polite conversation. It is an 'un-sexing' experience, in which a woman may feel less feminine and a man less virile, and thus it creates intense shame. There is a sense in which infertility is more closely related to disability than to illness. Infertile people cannot do something that most people expect to be able to do without help (Moss and Baden 2015, p. 4). Around the time we were having fertility treatment, our church rallied round to pray for a member who was having cancer treatment, and to offer support and care. I remember sitting in a meeting once while people gathered round to lay hands on him and to pray. It was wonderful to see, and yet it made me feel extremely lonely. I was shut out of this level of care because of the secrecy that surrounded my treatment. Some people experiencing childlessness do share their struggles publicly in church: it was different for me because I was a minister, and had to be careful how much I shared. I also had to negotiate with my husband what was acceptable to share. When a couple experience childlessness, it is often the case that one partner is less willing to share than the other, and this will affect how much can be discussed with others. Good pastoral practice needs to be aware of, and sensitive to, these issues. Pastoral carers will need to be led by the person or couple struggling with childlessness, who will have a sense of how much they are happy to be publicly known. Even when you have been entrusted with certain information, such as the dates of procedures, people going through fertility treatment may not appreciate being asked too many questions, particularly if the news is not good. Rather than calling to ask how treatment is progressing, much better to check in and say, 'we're thinking of you', without asking questions.

How do we encourage people to share struggles that are so intensely painful and private? In my experience, people are prepared to talk to you about a struggle if you are prepared to talk about it in church. When I spoke from the pulpit about my struggles with anxiety, people came to me and said, 'me too'. When I made a point of mentioning that I took anti-depressants, others were able to discuss their treatment with me. When I finally felt able to speak publicly about the pain of my childlessness, others came to me with their own stories. If you want people to trust you with their vulnerability, trust them with yours. If you want people to break a taboo, you must break it first, in public worship. Most ministers and worship leaders will not have direct experience of childlessness, and may not wish to speak publicly about it if they do. But talking about childlessness – for example, in the context of preaching, or pastoral prayers on Mothering Sunday – will give people permission to speak up if they want to.

Finally, pastoral carers need to understand that childlessness is a long, long journey. It takes place over years, not months. Generally, before any diagnostic tests take place, a couple will have been trying for a baby for at least a year. The process of testing and diagnosis can easily take another year, if not longer, with long delays between hospital appointments. Even once a referral has been made for assisted reproduction, such as IUI or IVF, there can be waiting lists for treatment, which cause further delays. IVF is not a quick process, with each cycle taking many weeks, and a minimum three-month wait between cycles for the body to recover. Individuals and couples who go on to consider adoption then enter another very lengthy process. At the time of writing, I have been trying to have a child for six and a half years. Childlessness has been part of my story for a very long time, with no end in sight yet.

Really excellent pastoral care will not only show love and support, but will also help people to make sense of their experiences before God. Caring Christians may instinctively wish to say something that will re-establish a sense of God's love, peace and order; indeed, they may feel that it is their duty to do so. Personally, I found that people's attempts to reassure me of

God's goodness and sovereignty jarred horribly with the way I was feeling. These remarks came across to me as scolding; as shutting me down; as trying to stop my experiences from disturbing a world order that made others feel safe, but which for me had been shattered. A Christian who experienced infertility many years ago explained to me: 'I needed people to "stare into the abyss with me" – to acknowledge the reality that we may never conceive and be willing to stay there with us. I also needed people who held hope for us when we couldn't hold on any more.'[4]

It was pastoral theology that eventually restored my faith in God's goodness and in the Christian story. As I read the Bible through the lens of my experience, I did find company. I found the Teacher of Ecclesiastes, crying out along with me at the senselessness of life, and challenging the smug certainties of the wisdom tradition. I found Rachel, crying out along with me, 'Give me children, or I shall die!' I found Ruth and Naomi, suffering appalling loss and financial ruin, and creating a new family that transcended biological ties, through love. And I found Jesus, lying dead in the tomb, sharing my brokenness; and then there, in the garden of resurrection, offering me hope. There is a great deal in the riches of the Bible and Christian tradition to offer companionship in suffering, as well as hope in the future.

Sometimes liturgy may be helpful for use during a pastoral visit, to help people experiencing infertility and childlessness to shape a conversation with God about their struggle. There are liturgical resources out there but you have to dig around a bit. Here are two excellent options:

- The Saltwater and Honey blog offers some helpful material: http://saltwaterandhoney.org/liturgies.
- *Women's Uncommon Prayers: Our Lives Revealed, Nurtured, Celebrated*, edited by Elizabeth Rankin Geitz, Marjorie A. Burke and Ann Smith (Morehouse Publishing), includes material covering infertility, miscarriage and menopause.

Sometimes people may be happy to pray with the pastoral visitor; at other times, the prayer may be left for them to reflect on and perhaps to pray on their own. I wrote the following prayer myself with a pastoral visit in mind. It could be used to name and hold before God the difficult feelings that may arise with a decision to stop fertility treatment:

Liturgy to mark the end of failed fertility treatment

In the case of an individual who has undertaken fertility treatment on their own, 'we' could still be used, as the one leading prayers identifies with the one who has suffered disappointment.

Loving God, we come to you with broken hearts.
We come to you, having tried and failed.
Like the woman who touched the fringe of your cloak,
we come to you, having spent much, and received nothing
    in return.

Compassionate God, we bring you our sorrow.
The many tears we have cried
The tears we have held back
The tears we did not want others to see
The tears we could not stop from flowing over.
We believe you have shared our sorrow.

Servant God, we bring you our powerlessness.
Our inability to bring about the future we wanted so much.
We feel weak and deeply frustrated.
We remember the time when you shared our weakness,
being born as a human baby.
We remember when you hung on the cross
and your weakness was mocked by the crowd.
We remember when you shared the ultimate weakness of
    death.

Holy God, we bring you our anger,
our deep sense of unfairness.
We acknowledge before you the outrage we feel
at being denied what others so easily achieve.
We confess the anger we have felt towards you,
and we ask for your mercy and help as we hold these
    feelings.

Merciful God, we are tired, and we know it is time to stop.
We come before you today to start saying goodbye
to the future for which we had hoped.
We place our shattered dreams
beside your still body in the tomb
trusting that, in time, you will bring resurrection.

And as we wait for the time when hope rises once more
hold us tightly, risen Lord,
And help us to hold tightly to you.

In Jesus' name,
Amen.

Section two: Some suggestions for public worship

In public worship, particularly at sensitive times of the year, we can use liturgy to name and include the experiences of people who may feel that they are on the margins. On Mothering Sunday, I have in the past explicitly prayed for people who long to be parents, along with people whose parents have died, or who have difficult family relationships. In the prayer offered below, I do not list all the painful situations that may come to people's minds on Mothers' Day or Fathers' Day. Instead I affirm that we are all part of human families, whether or not we have children, and whether or not our families are happy. All human families are broken to a greater or lesser extent, and we do not do anyone a favour by colluding with the 'Hallmark card' illusion of family harmony on Mothers' Day or Fathers'

Day. I believe it is important to acknowledge and to unpack what it means to be a church family, a family to which all can belong and that has the potential to offer what our human families do not:

A prayer for Mothers' Day and Fathers' Day

Mother and Father God,
we thank you for your love,
more tender than a human parent could ever offer.
Today we remember together mothers and fathers who have
    died
and we thank you for the life you gave us through them.
We thank you for our human families
for the messy intimacy
for the good-enough love we try to show each other
as we muddle along together.
We thank you too for our church family
as we too muddle along together,
parenting each other,
loving each other as best we can,
sometimes hurting each other,
and sometimes healing the wounds our biological families
have left behind.
Help us to love each other as you love us
In Jesus' name
Amen.

Easter

In Chapter 2 we dwelt at length on the cross, tomb and resurrection of Christ through the lens of involuntary childlessness. At Easter there are many opportunities to minister to people experiencing pain and struggle through preaching on Christ's death and resurrection.

Some Christian preachers will consider their principal duty

to call their congregations to repentance from sin. They will speak of the power of sin broken on the cross; they may declare that the penalty of sin was paid by Christ on our behalf. There is undoubtedly important truth to be found in penal substitutionary theories of the atonement, but I would question whether these theories are sufficient fully to address the needs of our congregations. We all need to understand the ways in which we estrange ourselves from God and contribute to the brokenness of the world by our ongoing selfishness. But not everything that drags people down is caused by sin. Pain and tragedy can also estrange us from God as our belief in God's power and God's goodness is profoundly undermined. By making room for theories of the atonement that announce God's solidarity with those who suffer, we may offer deep solace to people who are struggling to make sense of their pain before God. Serene Jones argues that different theories of the atonement will help different people, as we see our stories of suffering mirrored on the cross. She gives the example of a woman who had survived domestic abuse who imagined Jesus standing between her and her partner, taking the blows meant for her, and then holding her afterwards as she wept. Multiple theories of the atonement may be at work, as people make sense of their own trauma through the traumatic event of the cross (Jones 2009, p. 82).

During Holy Week in 2016 my church hosted an exhibition of the stations of the cross which featured photographs of refugees. By that time, my husband and I had been trying to conceive for over two years, and I was 36 years old. I was preparing myself for the fact that fertility treatment was inevitable. The refugees' stories of suffering were told as part of the exhibition, and one in particular stood out for me as I prepared to lead the Good Friday service. A pregnant woman was forced to flee the war in Syria, beginning the long journey on foot to relative safety in Lebanon. During the journey, her baby died in the womb, but weeks passed before she was able to get the medical treatment she needed.[5] This harrowing story reminded me powerfully of Serene Jones's image of death taken up into the Godhead, considered in Chapter 2. This Syrian lady carried her dead child within her body. God carried death within God-self when the eternal Son died on the cross.

I was not sure whether my congregation could cope with that image, however, much as it had helped me, so I made only a very passing allusion to it. Here is an extract from the sermon (written before I took up the discipline of avoiding the use of gendered pronouns for God):

> Jesus came to be with us. He lived among us. He lived as one of us. He shared our joys and he shared our agonies too. Like those who suffer depression, he too felt the pain of despair when all hope was gone. Like those who are sick, he too experienced bodily suffering too great to bear. Like those who are abused, he too was abused by others for their amusement, a person treated as a thing with no rights and no feelings. He, too, experienced death. The Father experienced what it was to lose a child. Suffering and even death were taken up into the Godhead. God carried death inside him. God took upon himself the terrible burden of sin, sorrow and brokenness of a hurting world. And because the Son of God was Godforsaken; because on that one day he felt what it was to have everything stripped away but his pain; because he was there in that darkness then, he is there always. Because he was there, we can never be alone in that dark place. There is no place where God is not.[6]

Christmas

Doubtless most pastors, preachers and church leaders are aware these days of the pastoral implications of Christmas. That at a time of compulsory jollity, those whose lives are marked by struggle can feel their pain most keenly. Of course, this is not always true – even at my saddest times, Christmas has never failed to cheer me up. But many find the enforced cheeriness jars horribly with their own sadness, loss and strug-gle. And yet the theological themes of Advent and Christmas can offer deep consolation.

Remember Advent

Clergy often bemoan the way in which everyone starts talking about 'Christmas' on 1 December, if not long before, ignoring the liturgical season of Advent altogether. Advent is a season that offers deep consolation for those who suffer deeply. Here is an Advent carol for those who suffer:

> O come, O come, Emmanuel,
> And ransom captive Israel,
> That mourns in lonely exile here,
> Until the Son of God appear.
> Rejoice! Rejoice! Emmanuel
> Shall come to thee, O Israel.
>
> O come, Thou Rod of Jesse, free
> Thine own from Satan's tyranny;
> From depths of hell Thy people save,
> And give them victory o'er the grave.
> Rejoice! Rejoice! Emmanuel
> Shall come to thee, O Israel.

Israel waits for release from captivity; for victory over the grave; for the dark shadows to disperse; for the way to the heavenly home. She waits for the Messiah to come and save. The theme of waiting may resonate deeply with people experiencing pain and struggle. The most powerful experience of preaching I have ever had came with a seven-minute talk I gave early one Advent Sunday morning many years ago. It was a sermon I wrote literally on the back of an envelope: not because I could not be bothered to prepare, but because what I needed to say was so clear to me that I only needed the briefest of notes. Afterwards I scribbled down more complete notes, and I have since tried preaching the same sermon, but it has never had the same effect. It was something that the Spirit did on that morning, in that moment. Essentially, I was speaking about waiting, and all the different things human beings wait for, from early childhood to the frailty of old age. Then I spoke about all the things people waited for in the Bible – and were never disappointed. Finally, I quoted the penultimate verse of Revelation:

> The one who testifies to these things says, 'Surely I am
>   coming soon.'
> Amen. Come, Lord Jesus! (Rev. 22.20)

Jesus says he is coming soon. And we call upon him to hurry: 'Come, Lord Jesus!' During the season of Advent we can bring to mind all the things for which we wait and hope. For healing, for the restoration of a relationship, for a child, for a job, for relief from pain. And we call upon the Lord Jesus to come quickly to help us.

Preachers may wish to develop this theme of waiting a little further. After all, we will not all see in our lifetimes the things for which we wait. Rosemary Morgan puts this well:

> When we first began our quest to become parents, my husband and I thought that was what we were doing – waiting for a child. As the quest became longer and the disappointments piled up on top of one another, waiting began to look like the wrong image. We are not waiting any longer. Now we are fighting, mourning, seeking, longing. Waiting for a baby is what we used to do. (Morgan 2013, p. 14)

Fighting, mourning, seeking, longing. These verbs all complement and enrich the image of waiting. Longing for something that may never come. Seeking for the blessing of God in the midst of disappointment. Fighting the odds, fighting against injustice. Mourning as the wait drags on and on with no end in sight. All this struggle can be contained within the Advent theme of waiting. At Christmas we celebrate the birth of Christ. Even for those of us not in much of a mood to celebrate, we can perhaps see Christmas Day as a foretaste of the more complete joy for which we still wait. Come quickly, Lord Jesus.

Some years ago, I preached on the story of Elizabeth and Zechariah at the late-night Christmas Eve communion service. The congregation had no idea of the particular resonance that story had for me at the time. I focused on the concept of remembering. God remembered Elizabeth and Zechariah; God heard Zechariah's prayer. Zechariah's name means 'God remembers'. There is potential here to touch upon themes of suffering, disappointment and struggle while preaching a Christmas text. This story ends with a miracle, of course, like (almost) all the other stories of infertility in the Bible. And yet, handled sensitively, this story could be used to name and to include the experiences of those who are still waiting for their prayers to be answered.

Not jollity, but joy

The Christian hope of Christmas is not that we may be jolly, but that we may know joy, although this can be lost amid the barrage of festive messages all around us. Through his concept 'Four Kinds of Christmas', the evangelist Glen Scrivener cleverly unpacks the different messages we receive and the different emotional reactions we may have to Christmas, explaining the way in which the true hope of the Bethlehem stable transcends them all. A 'Santa' Christmas is all about joy and happiness, he argues, but this kind of Christmas fails to acknowledge the difficult realities of pain and struggle. A 'Scrooge' Christmas acknowledges these painful realities, but offers no hope. A 'Shopper' Christmas is all about 'buy now, pay later' – seize a little happiness now and worry about it in January when the credit card bill comes in. Whereas a Christmas centred on the stable teaches us that, while pain and struggle are a reality now, there is joy to come.[7]

This way of understanding the interaction of sadness and joy, struggle and hope, has great potential to help people who find Christmas hard, including people struggling with childlessness. According to Scrivener, the Christian hope of Christmas lies precisely in a recognition that things are very difficult now – but that this will not always be the case. Christ came to us, born as a human baby. Christ will come again.

God with us, as one of us

The Christian story of Christmas centres on a baby, and this may be difficult for people struggling with childlessness. In 2010 an ecumenical Christmas campaign depicted a scan photo of the baby Jesus in the womb, complete with halo.[8] There are few images more viscerally painful for a person experiencing childlessness than someone else's ultrasound scan. Baby images aside, however, there may be healing potential in the notion that Christ chose to embrace the weakness and frailty of infancy to be with us. In Chapter 3 I explored the powerlessness experienced by people who want children and cannot have them; who may be used to a high degree of agency in their everyday lives and yet have no power to achieve the one thing they so desperately want. In Chapter 1 we considered the profound isolation experienced by people who struggle to have children when many around them achieve this easily. At Christmas we remember that God came to be with us, as one of us, sharing our weakness. These are themes that may be deeply therapeutic for people who feel that they are alone in their weakness, including people struggling with childlessness.

We turn now to the issue of all-age worship. How might we offer public worship that includes children, without alienating adults, especially those without children?

How to run an all-age service that childless people will not avoid

The all-age service can be a controversial thing. I have always loved all-age services, despite being a childless adult, and continue to advocate for their inclusion within church programmes for several reasons. First, because they help us all access playfulness, something that grieving people lose for a time, and need to get back. Jody Day writes of the importance of rediscovering creativity and play after grief (Day 2016, p. 257).

All-age services can provide a space for playfulness and creativity which allows the whole congregation to engage a different part of their brain and to receive new insights. This is closely related to my second reason for advocating all-age services, which is that they encourage experimentation with teaching and presentation styles that do not only benefit children. Good all-age services use creative, playful and interactive techniques to get across spiritual ideas and to keep everyone interested. Most churches rely most of the time on teaching techniques that, in educational circles, would be considered very outdated. We stand at the front, pouring knowledge from ourselves into the empty vessels of the congregants, asking only that they occasionally stand up or repeat some words of the liturgy. In teacher training in the early noughties I was taught never to speak for more than about five minutes without a break, and to break up lessons into chunks to keep children's interest. I would never have been able to indulge in a lengthy monologue and hold my class's attention. I suspect all people secretly have the attention span of an eight-year-old, we just get better at hiding it as we get older.

Third, all-age services promote inclusion. They force congregations to acknowledge and to try to meet the needs of younger members – but others can benefit from this inclusion too. I started going to church in my twenties with no previous background of churchgoing. I had very limited biblical and theological knowledge, and I found that the all-age services did not take for granted a lot of background knowledge that I, for one, did not have. These services did not assume I knew the broad sweep of Old Testament history; they did not assume I understood concepts like 'grace', 'salvation' and 'the kingdom of God'. But I did not grow out of all-age services, even once I had been to theological college. Having been taught the art of sermon-writing and delivery, I believe even more firmly now that simplicity and clarity are most important in preaching and teaching. And let us not fool ourselves that it is only the children who do not understand the big concepts and do not know the Bible inside out. Lots of adult churchgoers do not know these things either – they are just too ashamed to admit it.

A good sermon never says anything too complicated: it just tells a simple truth in a fresh way. Jesus loves you. God has forgiven you. God is with you. The Holy Spirit lives in you. I resist the notion that to make a service child-friendly means to dumb it down. Children can grasp profound truths: they just cannot grasp them in abstract language without a story or a prop or an example to help them. I believe passionately that all-age services are not just for children – and they are not just for families. Granted, I am sure that, in practice, these services often fail to engage adults who are not parents or grandparents. But I still believe in the possibility of a service that is interactive and creative enough to engage children without patronizing adults. Here are some suggestions for planning and delivering all-age services that childless people will not avoid.

Find people who have the skills and passion

I have had the privilege of serving as a volunteer, lay worker and minister in churches with very creative all-age worship teams. I realize that not all ministers and worship leaders have the skills or the desire to lead all-age worship. But I believe most churches have people who do have those skills, so my advice is: find them and let them loose. If you do not have enough volunteer capacity to manage a monthly all-age service, then do it quarterly. Some people have the confidence to stand up at the front of the church and lead. Others have the creative skills to put a game or drama together or to create some props. Some have the gift of getting people of all ages to join in, using musical instruments, signing or simple actions. There are many different skills that can come together to create a great all-age service.

Experiment with formats

There are lots of different formats you can use to deliver a great all-age service. You can offer a modified version of a front-led service, but with shorter chunks of singing, teaching and prayers to create more variety. You can build in interactive games and drama, being sure to use adults as well as children. Try to resist the notion that the adults are sitting there watching something being delivered for children. If you are asking for volunteers, include a mix of ages.

You could be more creative still and break the congregation into groups for different activities. If you have a building with a number of meeting spaces, you could offer a traditional Bible discussion in one room, a craft or cooking activity related to the theme in another, and perhaps a creative prayer station in a third. In the past I have used the Messy Church format on a Sunday morning, with everyone in the congregation moving around activity tables (though I will confess that many older adults and those preferring a more traditional form of worship struggled). When I was part of a church-planting team with a lot of unaccompanied children in the congregation, I once built a 'burning bush' in the middle of the room, which we sat around with our shoes off. This turned the whole worship space into the set of the story. Much will depend upon the space available and the tolerance levels of the congregation – but this is also where education comes in.

Educate the congregation

Be explicit about what you are trying to do and why. I have made mistakes in the past where I have conducted creative experiments without explaining my rationale. Many people simply do not believe that anything other than an exegetical monologue will feed their discipleship. Anything involving drama, craft or games, or requiring people to build their own sermon, are seen as dumbing down. Challenge this. Explain that a sermon is an opportunity to meet with God. Point out that it is not when we acquire head knowledge but when we put our learning into practice that we are truly following Christ. And remind the congregation that there are people of all ages and abilities in the church family, some of whom are routinely shuttled out into separate rooms for Sunday school so that the adults can get on with 'proper church'. All-age worship enables children and young people to know that they are valued members of the fellowship.

Actively include people of all family circumstances

The most reliable way of planning an all-age service that will not alienate single and childless people is to involve them in the planning and delivery. Commit to a service that is truly inclusive of all ages, not simply a service with something for the kids. Think multi-generational worship. Have people of all family circumstances saying prayers, running activities and giving talks (ideally talks should be no more than five to seven minutes long).

Tackle Mothering Sunday and Father's Day head on. Some people may choose to stay away, and they should be free to do so, but a well-thought-out all-age service may give them the option of turning up. As part of a Mother's or Father's Day service, emphasize the role of the whole congregation in bringing up children and sharing their faith with them.

One particular bone of contention is the phrase 'family service', often used to denote an all-age service. Some argue that this sends the message that single and childless people are not welcome. But I still have a family, even though I am childless. And I am still part of the church family. I suspect that the name by which the service is known matters less than the way in which it is planned and delivered. It may be that a church decides to have a 'family service' and to explain directly, from the front, every time, that this is a service for the whole church family. If the family services regularly include people of all ages and family circumstances saying prayers, running activities and giving talks, then the service will simply reinforce the message that everyone is part of this church family, regardless of their personal family circumstances.

Section three: Suggestions for preaching

> Helping people of faith find a tale of compassion and grace in the stories of God's good news, a story capable of giving manageable shape to their many griefs and angers – this is central to the pastor's more intimate role as counselor and guide to the broken and the searching. (Jones 2009, p. 90)

It may not be appropriate to preach specifically on the theme of childlessness very often, if ever. Many of the themes explored in previous chapters, however, have resonance far beyond simply those who remain involuntarily childless. In reading the Bible through the lens of childlessness, we have considered isolation, pain, powerlessness, barrenness and guilt. Pain and powerlessness, in particular, are universal themes. None of us can live without pain; none of us can control every aspect of our lives all the time, or even much of the time. Here I offer some suggestions for preachers who are seeking to help their congregations understand life's difficult experiences before God and in the context of their faith.

The story of Ruth

We considered this story in Chapter 1, as we looked for company for people struggling with childlessness in the Scriptures. There is material for a whole series in this little book of four chapters. There are themes around refugees and care for poor and marginalized people. There is wonder here, as a poor Moabite widow becomes the great-grandmother of King David, and ancestor of Jesus Christ himself. The story of Ruth and Naomi is one of a very small handful of Old Testament texts that tell women's stories without creating a significant problem for female readers of the Bible.[9] The book of Ruth is not only named after a woman, but is written almost entirely from a female perspective. Although Boaz, in marrying Ruth, 'redeems' Elimelech's inheritance and saves the women from poverty, it is the women who take the initiative in the story.

Ruth is a story for all those who are treated cruelly by life and who struggle against considerable odds. It is a story for those who feel utterly powerless against forces beyond their control. It is a story for those who are weak or marginalized; for those who are 'empty'.

Honesty about tragedy

Naomi suffers a terrible human tragedy, losing not just her husband but her children to early death (Ruth 1.1–4). This was not only emotionally devastating, but economically disastrous in a patriarchal society in which women depended on fathers, husbands and sons for survival. Naomi is not quiet and resigned; she is bitter and defeated:

> 'Call me no longer Naomi,
>   call me Mara,
>   for the Almighty has dealt bitterly with me.
> I went away full,
>   but the LORD has brought me back empty;
> why call me Naomi
>   when the LORD has dealt harshly with me,
>   and the Almighty has brought calamity upon me?'
> (Ruth 1.20–21)

How very uncomfortable acquaintances and friends alike might have felt, hearing Naomi's woes. No faith-filled platitudes here: only raw, deep sorrow. In Naomi's eyes, her misfortunes are all down to God and, while she might accept them, she is not resigned and nor is she peaceful. There is powerful material here for the preacher to affirm the sorrow, the bitterness, even the anger, people in the congregation may feel about the way their lives have turned out. Here there is permission to be fiercely angry, to be deeply sad, to blame God without holding back.

Love beyond the nuclear family

In the midst of the bitterness and the tragedy, however, there is great love. Ruth's devotion to her mother-in-law is even more touching for being perhaps unexpected. Naomi is not her mother, and can offer her nothing. It would be in Ruth's best interests to return home to her own mother and to enjoy the protection of her wider family. As a widow, Naomi is facing penury and, it seems, is too old for the hope of a new husband. And yet, Ruth loves her and will not leave her:

> 'Do not press me to leave you
>> or to turn back from following you!
> Where you go, I will go;
>> where you lodge, I will lodge;
> your people shall be my people,
>> and your God my God.
> Where you die, I will die –
>> there will I be buried.
> May the LORD do thus and so to me,
>> and more as well,
> if even death parts me from you!'
> When Naomi saw that she was determined to go with her, she said no more to her. (Ruth 1.16–18)

Ruth shares Naomi's desolation, becoming an economic refugee. She travels back to Judah with Naomi, in search of food. In Chapter 1 we explored briefly the ways in which churches can offer an understanding of family that transcends biology. Churches are communities bound together by the love of Christ. There are undoubtedly times when both single and childless people can feel alienated by the focus on families with children, but it does not have to be this way. Ruth loved her mother-in-law, and refused to leave her, even though she was not biologically related; even when there was no social pressure to stay with her; even when it was in her best interests to leave.

Taking action

We usually preach resignation to the will of God and trust in the Almighty for provision and protection. As we saw in Chapter 1, however, Ruth is not demure, she is not resigned, and neither is Naomi. They are not yet ready to lie down and be crushed by life. They stand up and fight for themselves. It seems that Boaz is aware of Naomi's tragedy, of Ruth's faithfulness to her, and of his kinship to Elimelech, Naomi's dead husband. And yet he has not taken the initiative to help the women: it is only when Ruth comes and puts herself in a compromising position on the threshing-floor that Boaz is prompted to do what he can as kinsman-redeemer. There is a time for quiet trust and resignation, but perhaps there is also a time for taking action. Ruth's actions on the threshing-floor might almost be seen as an act of protest against her poverty. Boaz has the means to help her, but so far has done nothing. Ruth puts herself in his power and, in doing so, prompts him to protect and to help her.

Restoration

On one level, this is the story of two women who need a man to save them – a story of two widows who need marriage to be made whole. This is the story of one woman whose children have died, and another whose husband died before any children were conceived – and the happy ending comes with a baby. Certainly, baby Obed brings great joy and celebration. He is not genetically Naomi's grandson: and yet, as Boaz has redeemed Elimelech's inheritance, he stands in the place of the grandchildren Naomi never had. The family line is restored by marriage and by the birth of a baby.

And yet, if we consider the words of 'the women' to Naomi at the end of the story, it is clear that Ruth is just as much part of Naomi's happy ending as her child:

> Then the women said to Naomi, 'Blessed be the LORD, who has not left you this day without next-of-kin; and may his name be renowned in Israel! He shall be to you a restorer of life and a nourisher of your old age; for your daughter-in-law who loves you, who is more to you than seven sons, has borne him.' (Ruth 4.14–15)

This young woman has shared Naomi's tragedy; she has even shared her desolation. She has become a refugee and been a companion in Naomi's struggle for survival. Naomi has lost much, but she has gained a daughter, 'more to you than seven sons'. There is surely tremendous grace here for those of us whose families do not look like other people's; those of us whose families are created through love and friendship rather than biology. There is tremendous promise: that despite adversity, despite tragedy, love may come to us in unexpected forms.

The story of Ruth and Naomi offers the comfort of a happy ending. We now consider the book of Ecclesiastes, part of the body of work called the wisdom writings. This book is unflinchingly honest about the uncomfortable realities of life, and yet we may find solace precisely in its honesty.

Ecclesiastes

We considered Ecclesiastes in Chapter 4, where I suggested the word 'barren' as a possible translation of the Hebrew word *hebel*. We now consider the use of Ecclesiastes in preaching. This book is a precious gift to all those whose suffering makes them ask questions. It has been described as the 'ghost at the banquet' of the biblical canon (Kaiser 1995, p. 84). Some see the Teacher in Ecclesiastes as writing in protest against the wisdom tradition.[10] Where established wisdom tells us that those who wisely fear God prosper and have many children, and the foolish perish, the Teacher declares:

> vanity of vanities! All is vanity.
> What do people gain from all the toil
>   at which they toil under the sun?
> (Eccles. 1.2–3)

The Teacher in Ecclesiastes shoots from the hip. All of life, he declares, is 'vanity'.

Honesty about tragedy

The Teacher is searingly honest about the painful experiences of life:

> ... it is an unhappy business that God has given to human beings to be busy with. (Eccles. 1.13b)

> Again I saw all the oppressions that are practised under the sun. Look, the tears of the oppressed – with no one to comfort them! On the side of their oppressors there was power – with no one to comfort them. And I thought the dead, who have already died, more fortunate than the living, who are still alive; but better than both is the one who has not yet been, and has not seen the evil deeds that are done under the sun. (Eccles. 4.1–3)

The Teacher sees so much suffering that he radically denies life's goodness (Crenshaw 2010, p. 130). The person who is never born is more fortunate than those who are living. Life 'is an unhappy business'. Mourning and sorrow are better, says the Teacher, than joy and laughter:

> A good name is better than precious ointment,
>   and the day of death, than the day of birth.
> It is better to go to the house of mourning
>   than to go to the house of feasting;
> for this is the end of everyone,
>   and the living will lay it to heart.
> Sorrow is better than laughter,
>   for by sadness of countenance the heart is made glad.
> The heart of the wise is in the house of mourning;
>   but the heart of fools is in the house of mirth.
> (Eccles. 7.1–4)

Perhaps it is simply that mourning and sorrow are more familiar to the Teacher than feasting and laughter. People who are struggling sometimes do not feel that they fit into groups of people who are celebrating. The mood of mourning is a better fit – it expresses how they feel about life.

The Teacher sees, not only sorrow, but senselessness:

> Again I saw that under the sun the race is not to the swift, nor the battle to the strong, nor bread to the wise, nor riches to the intelligent, nor favour to the skilful; but time and chance happen to them all. For no one can anticipate the time of disaster. Like fish taken in a cruel net, and like birds caught in a snare, so mortals are snared at a time of calamity, when it suddenly falls upon them. (Eccles. 9.11–12)

The fastest person does not win the race; the strongest does not win the battle; prosperity does not come to the wise, intelligent and skilful person. Everyone is subject to blind chance. This is certainly true of infertility and childlessness. While there is an element of predictability – youth and health give you a better chance of conception – ultimately no one can predict whether a person will be able to have a child. The gift of Ecclesiastes for those who suffer is a companion in pain.

The Teacher has a residual sense that life should be just – there is a real ambivalence here about the way in which life does, or does not, make sense:

> Then I saw the wicked buried; they used to go in and out of the holy place, and were praised in the city where they had done such things. This also is vanity. Because sentence against an evil deed is not executed speedily, the human heart is fully set to do evil. (Eccles. 8.10–11)

He declares, however, that the wicked will not prevail:

> Though sinners do evil a hundred times and prolong their lives, yet I know that it will be well with those who fear God, because they stand in fear before him, but it will not be well with the wicked, neither will they prolong their days like a shadow, because they do not stand in fear before God. (Eccles. 8.12–13)

And then immediately changes his mind again:

> There is a vanity that takes place on earth, that there are righteous people who are treated according to the conduct of the wicked, and there are wicked people who are treated according to the conduct of the righteous. I said that this also is vanity. (Eccles. 8.14)

This ambivalence may be very familiar to those of us who struggle. We believe that God is just and that life makes sense, and yet our experiences cause us to doubt. We have not yet entirely let go of this belief in order, and so we are in two minds – perhaps like the father who declared, 'I do believe; help me overcome my unbelief' (Mark 9.24).

The Teacher concludes this swithering by declaring mystery:

> When I applied my mind to know wisdom, and to see the business that is done on earth, how one's eyes see sleep neither day nor night, then I saw all the work of God, that no one can find out what is happening under the sun. However much they may toil in seeking, they will not find it out; even though those who are wise claim to know, they cannot find it out. (Eccles. 8.16–17)

Living life now

There is a resolution of sorts in Ecclesiastes – the response of the Teacher to this painful – and apparently senseless – mystery is to declare that we should all enjoy life while we can:

> Go, eat your bread with enjoyment, and drink your wine with a merry heart; for God has long ago approved what you do. Let your garments always be white; do not let oil be lacking on your head. Enjoy life with the wife whom you love, all the days of your vain life that are given you under the sun, because that is your portion in life and in your toil at which you toil under the sun. Whatever your hand finds to do, do with your might; for there is no work or thought or knowledge or wisdom in Sheol, to which you are going. (Eccles. 9.7–10)

Some skill is required to interpret this message for followers of Jesus. The writer of Ecclesiastes did not have a concept of life beyond death, and hence hope had to be here and now. He urges his readers to enjoy life while they can: to eat and drink, to cherish their life partner, and to work hard at whatever it is they do.

There is no resurrection in the Teacher's worldview but there is, I think, much wisdom in the advice he gives. After all, we are embodied creatures. We not only need food and drink to survive but we have the gift of being able to enjoy these things. We need relationships and we need work to give our lives enjoyment, purpose and meaning. Part of the toll childlessness can take is the obsession with something we do not yet have; the constant looking to the future and the hoped-for child. Sometimes people come to the realization that it will be better for them and for their relationships to stop trying and start living. They realize how much they are losing from life right now because of the blessing that has been denied. Ecclesiastes does not encompass all of Christian hope, but it offers the wisdom that life is to be lived right now.

We turn now to the New Testament. Shortly, we will look at the resurrection, but first we will focus on Holy Saturday, sometimes thought of as the in-between day between Good Friday and Easter Sunday. The pain of Holy Saturday was considered at length in Chapter 2, but here we return to its use in preaching.

Holy Saturday

On Holy Saturday, nothing happens. Matthew tells us that the chief priests and Pharisees ask Pilate to seal the tomb, so that the disciples cannot steal Jesus' body and claim resurrection (Matt. 27.62–66). But other than that, Jesus' story seems to be over: he is dead and in the tomb:

> When it was evening, there came a rich man from Arimathea, named Joseph, who was also a disciple of Jesus. He went to

Pilate and asked for the body of Jesus; then Pilate ordered it to be given to him. So Joseph took the body and wrapped it in a clean linen cloth and laid it in his own new tomb, which he had hewn in the rock. He then rolled a great stone to the door of the tomb and went away. Mary Magdalene and the other Mary were there, sitting opposite the tomb. (Matt. 27.57–61)

We preach on the cross frequently; we reassure our people that their sins are forgiven, their shame is wiped out, that they can never be alone in their sorrows, as Christ has shared pain and abandonment and death. We preach on the resurrection frequently; we remind our people that death is not the end, that our greatest enemy has been defeated, that Christ has turned the grave from a dead end into a thoroughfare. But I have never heard a sermon on Holy Saturday. It is a pause. What can be said about it to help our people? 'The nonevent of the second day could after all be a *significant* zero, a *pregnant* emptiness, a silent nothing which says *everything*' (Lewis 2001, p. 3).

Holy Saturday speaks to chronic pain, unglamorous suffering

We all have crises in our lives. Some have greater and more frequent crises than others. We all get sick; we all experience loss; we all, from time to time, have to deal with emergencies. We all, at times, will have to deal with acute pain. Acute pain is short, sharp pain – it is very unpleasant while it lasts, but it does not last for ever. Chronic pain is different. Chronic pain goes on and on and on. It can be physical pain, such as debilitating arthritis or back pain. It can also be emotional – such as the pain of grief that remains after the initial shock has worn off. We are most familiar with grief when it applies to people we love who have died, but we can grieve other things too. We can grieve the loss of a friendship or family relationship that has gone sour. We can grieve the loss of a career that illness or redundancy or family circumstances have taken away from us.

We can grieve for something we never had, such as a child or a marriage or a parent we never met.

Our lives do not always turn out the way we expected, hoped and dreamed, and sometimes the pain goes on and on. Holy Saturday is a day for people who live with pain. For people whose hopes have died. For people who continue to suffer once the crisis is over and everyone else has moved on. On Holy Saturday we remember that Christ died and, for a time, he stayed dead. He did not jump triumphantly from the cross to the garden of resurrection. Some versions of the Apostles' Creed state that Christ 'descended to the dead' or even 'descended into hell'. We can tie ourselves in knots trying to understand 'where' Christ was during this time: the important thing is that he was in the tomb, and he was dead. This is not a pleasant thought, but it is a strange kind of comfort to those of us who live with pain and loss. Those of us who have not yet glimpsed hope can rest with Christ in the tomb, where our pain is made holy (Ellis 2006, p. 25).

Holy Saturday contains our ugliness

Christ was really human; he had a real human body; he really died. In the story of the raising of Lazarus in John 11 the bystanders were reluctant to roll away the stone because they knew Lazarus' body would have started to decay. Christ's body, too, would have started to decompose. This is one of the crude realities of being an embodied human being: we are sweaty, we are hairy, we are smelly and, after we die, we smell even worse. We shower and shave and use deodorant to make ourselves presentable much of the time, but the intimate realities of our bodies are not glamorous. And Christ shared our physical humanity: our sweaty, hairy, smelly reality. When he died, his body started to decompose as one day ours will too.

Our bodies are not always presentable, and the same is true for our emotions. Especially when we are in distress, our emotions are not pretty. Most of the time, we are all right with happiness, excitement and love, and we can probably cope with a little sadness and a little anger – especially if it is righteous anger. But what about envy? What about anger that someone else has something we do not think they deserve – something for which we have longed and prayed and been endlessly disappointed? What about bitterness and cynicism – the kind of weary protest that is all we have the energy for, once our anger has burned out? What about the kind of sadness that is utterly draining and debilitating to be around – both for the person who is sad and for the people all around them?

Perhaps Christ's body in the tomb in all its unglamorous decomposition might remind us that we do not have to tidy ourselves up for God. That God knows every detail, both pretty and ugly, and all is contained in the love of God.

Holy Saturday is the place for those things we are waiting for God to raise

If God can raise the dead body of Christ, then God can raise anything. The beautiful poem 'Seven Stanzas at Easter' by John Updike speaks of God reversing the cells' dissolution, re-knitting the molecules, re-kindling the amino acids of Christ's body. If God can take Christ's dead body and breathe life back into it, then God can raise all that is dead within us too. But while we are still in the season of hopelessness, we can leave those things in the tomb, awaiting the breath of God.

It is axiomatic that we live in the pause between 'now' and 'not yet'. The kingdom is both here and not-yet-here. The power of sin has been broken, and yet we are still sinned against and sinning. Death has been defeated, and yet we still die. Christ rose, the firstfruits of the general resurrection (1 Cor. 15.20–23). And while we wait, the tomb of Holy Saturday can hold those things that so desperately need to be raised. The tomb of Holy Saturday holds a space for the tension between now and not yet.

Resurrection: the shorter ending of Mark (16.1–8)

This shorter ending (16.1–8) of Mark's Gospel tells the story of the resurrection without tidying up or providing resolution. When the women go to the tomb and find it empty, they are terrified, and run away in fear. We have already explored the notion of resurrection and its healing potential for people struggling with childlessness. In considering the broader category of survivors of trauma, Serene Jones is drawn to the shorter ending of Mark's Gospel. For Jones, this is a 'non-ending' (Jones 2009, pp. 85f.).

> When the sabbath was over, Mary Magdalene, and Mary the mother of James, and Salome bought spices, so that they might go and anoint him. And very early on the first day of the week, when the sun had risen, they went to the tomb. They had been saying to one another, 'Who will roll away the stone for us from the entrance to the tomb?' When they looked up, they saw that the stone, which was very large, had already been rolled back. As they entered the tomb, they saw a young man, dressed in a white robe, sitting on the right side; and they were alarmed. But he said to them, 'Do not be alarmed; you are looking for Jesus of Nazareth, who was crucified. He has been raised; he is not here. Look, there is the place they laid him. But go, tell his disciples and Peter that he is going ahead of you to Galilee; there you will see him, just as he told you.' So they went out and fled from the tomb, for terror and amazement had seized them; and they said nothing to anyone, for they were afraid. (Mark 16.1–8)

When I was young, I hated this kind of ending. I had little patience with ambiguity, with unresolved issues and questions. I wanted a happy ending, or at least a redemptive ending, with all loose ends tied up. As I moved into my thirties, and even more so as my own struggles with infertility and childlessness became apparent, I started to find myself drawn to this kind of unresolved ending. Stories told in popular books and films will usually have a story arc whereby some kind of tension or difficulty or crisis is resolved at the end. Perhaps one of the reasons detective fiction is so popular is precisely because of the comforting promise that, at the end, we will know all the answers and the murderer will be brought to justice. Romantic comedies end with a couple getting together. And yet, of course, we know that life is not really like this. We know that love sometimes goes unrequited; killers are not brought to justice; questions remain unanswered. We all live in the middle of our stories, and the tensions can be deeply uncomfortable.

How does the Christian story help us resolve this tension? We have already heard of the many ways in which people try to resolve the experiences of childless people in ways that might seem pious but that can be deeply unhelpful. And, of course, these well-meaning, unhelpful pieties are not only inflicted on childless people, but on all those whose stories fail to follow the 'prescribed script'. An illness is followed, ideally by a healing or, failing that, by a deep spiritual insight that makes it all worthwhile. A bereavement is managed with quiet tears behind closed doors. A redundancy is followed by a new job that is supplied just at the right time. Rosemary Morgan expresses well the way in which her experience of infertility failed to follow the prescribed script:

> Everyone would have preferred it if I had had a miracle baby. It would have made everybody's life easier.[11]

When the healing does not come, the spiritual insight proves elusive, the new job cannot be found and the tears are too loud, the pieties are brought out. If there is still hope, we are told that God is in control and will resolve the problem. If there is no longer hope, we are told that God has a bigger purpose that we cannot see. We are reminded that God is good. We are discouraged from questioning God's bigger purpose, from questioning God's goodness. This painful, questioning, grey area is deeply uncomfortable and many are unwilling to share the discomfort.

But right here in the Bible we have an unresolved story. The greatest story ever told, in fact, is left hanging. The women are told that Christ has been raised, and that they should tell the disciples. But they run away in fear. We are left with questions. Who will tell the disciples that Christ is risen? Why have the women received such good news with such terror? Are they not meant to be the most faithful ones – the ones who did not run away, but stayed with Jesus until the end, and are now here to serve him in death? Early editors of Mark's Gospel dealt with this in one of two ways. In some cases, a couple of sentences were added to wrap up the story:

> And all that had been commanded them they told briefly to those around Peter. And afterward Jesus himself sent out through them, from east to west, the sacred and imperishable proclamation of eternal salvation.

In other manuscripts, verses 9–20 are added to finish off the story in a more satisfying way. In these verses we read of Jesus' appearances to Mary Magdalene and to two disciples on the road to Emmaus, who tell the eleven, but are not believed. Finally, Jesus appears to the eleven and sends them out to proclaim the good news.

Even in the biblical text, then, we see this discomfort with unfinished stories – this desire to wrap things up neatly. And yet, it seems that the original author of Mark was not afraid of a messy ending. And so perhaps the messy ending of Mark might authorize us to hold our own and one another's unfinished stories. To acknowledge that some things are unknown; sometimes we suffer with no ending; sometimes people's feelings do not fit into the expected pattern.

The 2018 Netflix film *Private Life* has an ending that brilliantly expresses the reality of journeying with infertility and childlessness. In the last scene, an infertile couple are sitting in a diner waiting to meet a young woman who is looking for adoptive parents for her child. The camera lingers on them as they fidget and wait. We know that they have been disappointed in the past. They were once put in touch with a young woman who seemed keen that they adopt her unborn child, only for her to disappear, breaking off all contact. They have been told that sometimes young women pretend to be pregnant because they enjoy the attention. The couple have tried IVF using donor eggs and it has been unsuccessful: it seems adoption is their only chance of having a child. And so they wait, as the credits roll, to see if the woman will turn up this time. As someone who has experienced much disappointment and has endured much waiting, I find this a deeply satisfying ending, because it is so honest. I have had many people tell me miracle baby stories, thinking they are being helpful, but I have always known that the miracle might never come. This film acknowledges the waiting, the uncertainty, not knowing if the treatment will ever work; if the birth mother will ever turn up. This is the reality. And the shorter ending of Mark affirms and holds that reality.

Section four: Resources

Below is a summary of the books and websites I have found most helpful. Some can be given to people experiencing childlessness; others are probably more suitable reading for those supporting them.

Books

Jody Day, 2016, *Living the Life Unexpected: How to Find Hope, Meaning and a Fulfilling Future* Without *Children*, London: Pan Macmillan.
This is a workbook for women who are coming to the realization that they will never have children. Day is a psychotherapist and a childless woman herself, and writes thoughtfully and helpfully about the grieving process as well as offering very practical ways of moving forward. Be aware, however, that this is a book for people who have given up hope of a child. It may not be appropriate for people who are contemplating further treatment, or looking to explore adoption.

Sally Donovan, 2013, *No Matter What: An Adoptive Family's Story of Hope, Love and Healing*, London: Jessica Kingsley.
A searingly honest account of Sally Donovan's infertility and her decision, along with her husband, to adopt two children. It is unflinching in its portrayal of the difficulties of parenting young, traumatized children, and would be a good read for a person or couple considering adoption following childlessness.

Kevin Ellis, 2006, *Christianity and Childlessness*, Cambridge: Grove Books.
A quick read and an excellent introduction to the topic. Ellis is deeply honest about the pain and the struggle. This would be useful for people experiencing childlessness as well as those seeking to support them.

Serene Jones, 2009, *Trauma and Grace: Theology in a Ruptured World*, Louisville, KY: Westminster John Knox Press.
This book considers trauma in general, but has a chapter on reproductive loss that is deeply moving and an outstanding piece of pastoral theology. It may be too hard a read for people whose experience of childlessness is raw, however, and may be more suitable reading for preachers seeking to understand this kind of loss in theological terms.

Lizzie Lowrie, 2020, *Salt Water and Honey: Lost Dreams, Good Grief and a Better Story*, Milton Keynes: Authentic.
A memoir in which Lizzie Lowrie describes the agony of six miscarriages and her painful attempts to keep going with God through it all. Lowrie is deeply honest and vulnerable, although the book could be triggering for people with recent experience of miscarriage. It would be excellent reading for those seeking to support others.

Rosemary Morgan, 2013, *Living with Infertility – a Christian Perspective*, Abingdon: The Bible Reading Fellowship.
A devotional book for people experiencing infertility. Rosemary Morgan draws on her own experience and is honest about the pain and struggle.

Mary Warnock, 2002, *Making Babies: Is There a Right to Have Children?*, Oxford: Oxford University Press.
This short book considers some of the ethical issues surrounding fertility treatment. It provides no answers, but I found it helpful for framing the ethical issues surrounding IVF.

Professor Robert Winston, 2015, *The Essential Fertility Guide*, London: Quadrille.
A must-read for people experiencing infertility or contemplating fertility treatment. Professor Winston explains with wisdom and compassion the causes of infertility and the various diagnostic tests and treatments available. This book could also be useful for pastoral carers who are helping people navigate the ethical dilemmas, and who need a detailed understanding of the medical procedures involved.

Websites

https://fertilitynetworkuk.org
www.miscarriageassociation.org.uk
These websites have lots of information about the practical and medical issues as well as the emotional aspects of miscarriage and infertility.

http://saltwaterandhoney.org
https://chasingcreation.org
These blogs thoughtfully explore the emotional impact of infertility and childlessness. Saltwater and Honey is from an explicitly Christian perspective. I found Chasing Creation to be excellent too.

www.robinhadley.co.uk
Robin Hadley is one of the few people writing about male infertility and its emotional impact. His work is commended by Jody Day.

https://infertileaf.libsyn.com

The title of this podcast – *Infertile AF* – just made me smile, although it is probably not suitable for anyone offended by swearing. Ali Prato interviews a different person each week about their story of infertility. Most interviewees are speaking from the US context, where fertility treatment is even more costly than it is in the UK, and the adoption process is very different. I appreciated the honesty and candour – although most of the stories end with a baby, and this may be difficult for people who are coming to terms with permanent childlessness. Prato's interviewees include women and men, LGBT+ people as well as heterosexuals and single people, as well as those in relationships.

Notes

1 Richard Foster, quoted in Voysey 2013, p. 44.

2 See Ellis 2006, p. 4, and McGuinness 1995, p. 223.

3 This is the one significant flaw in his work, in my opinion – it is a passing remark he makes in chapter four. I would hesitate to recommend this excellent book to people who had experienced miscarriage or stillbirth for this reason.

4 From private correspondence.

5 See https://thestations.org.uk/exhibitions/, accessed 17.1.2021.

6 The sermon drew heavily on the work of Jürgen Moltmann.

7 Glen Scrivener, 2015, *Four Kinds of Christmas*, Leyland: 10Publishing. The video 'Four Kinds of Christmas' is available at http://fourkindsofchristmas.com, accessed 7.3.2021.

8 Karen McVeigh, 2010, 'Church poster showing Jesus in the womb criticised as seeming "pro-life"', *The Guardian*, 9 June, www.theguardian.com/world/2010/jun/09/church-ad-campaign-jesus-womb, accessed 7.3.2021.

9 I love the Old Testament, and yet women's stories found there can be very hard to read. We may try to explain away the difficulties, but we cannot surely deny that they are there.

10 See, for example, Crenshaw 2010, pp. 127–31.

11 Quoted in Robin Gill, 2014, 'Fertility treatment and God', *Church Times*, 2 May, www.churchtimes.co.uk/articles/2014/2-may/features/features/fertility-treatment-and-god, accessed 7.3.2021.

Conclusion

In a 2013 interview, shame researcher Brené Brown describes an incident where she feared she had made a research error. In going over the notes of interviews with women who had discussed their infertility, she noticed that in every case the experience was recounted in the past tense. She went back and contacted a random sample of these women to check that their interviews had been logged correctly. In every case, they explained, 'I can't speak for the other women you've interviewed, but in the midst of my struggle I could have never talked to you about it. I could only talk to you about it because I've come to some resolution.'[1]

In February 2015, I started the journal that eventually became this book. By that point, I had been trying unsuccessfully to conceive for just over a year. In the first entry, I reflected on how easy it seemed to be for other people to get pregnant – and yet I realized that all I was seeing was a person with a baby. I had no idea how long that baby had taken to conceive, or what difficulties there might have been, because this is not the sort of thing people talk about. I wrote:

> I'm certainly not planning on publishing this ... until I'm pregnant, or until I give up hope. I don't want people asking me if we've had any luck yet, or asking intrusive questions about our sex life. I can't bear the thought of an audience while I'm going through the monthly cycle of hope, despair and renewed hope.

I looked forward with anticipation to the day that I would be able triumphantly to publish my journal as a blog post, ending with a pregnancy announcement. That day never came. Instead I acquired a readers' card for the British Library and began writing this book in earnest.

Then, with the adoption process came renewed hope, and I anticipated that my children would finally arrive, after all this time, just as I finished the manuscript. I felt as if I would be able to present my story from a place of resolution and happiness after all. This, too, will not happen. I write these words less than a fortnight before I am due to submit this manuscript to my publishers, and there is no end in sight – our adoption journey goes on and on. This story resists being neatly tied up.

Some things have been lost for ever. I do not pray the way I used to pray. I do not contemplate other people's tragedies in the detached way I used to, secure in my relative comfort and able to sympathize from a distance. I no longer believe that God is in control. I am wounded. And just when I think the wound has healed and become a scar, something happens and it reopens, raw and bleeding, and the serenity I thought I had finally achieved is stripped away.

At first, I insisted that I was not angry with God, only at the fertile world. Then I realized that I was furious with God. Now my fury is still there, but it is directed elsewhere. My anger is not directed at God any more, but at the bad theology and the insensitive practices that can prevent people from knowing the boundless love of God poured out on the cross, a love that longs to embrace all people along with their pain, terror and rage. When we tell people God is in control, what they often hear is that God is causing their pain. When we tell people to trust God, they realize they must dry their tears and cool their rage – because these feelings are not acceptable. When we tell only stories of triumph in the face of adversity, what people hear is that, unless they have a happy ending to offer, they must keep quiet.

What if all our feelings were acceptable to God? What if we embraced weakness and vulnerability as more Christlike than strength and success? What if we worked hard to seek a vision of 'church family' that truly included, loved and supported all people? What if we deliberately sought out uncomfortable, unfinished stories? What if we practised lament together? A Christian community like this would not only benefit people struggling with childlessness. It would enable all people who struggle – and, of course, *all* people struggle – to know that they need not hide their brokenness and rage in an attempt to fit in.

Several years ago, a visiting preacher delivered a sermon in my church entitled: 'When did we forget that church is for broken people?' The text was the parable of the Pharisee and the tax collector from Luke 18:

'Two men went up to the temple to pray, one a Pharisee and the other a tax collector. The Pharisee, standing by himself, was praying thus, "God, I thank you that I am not like other people: thieves, rogues, adulterers, or even like this tax collector. I fast twice a week; I give a tenth of all my income." But the tax collector, standing far off, would not even look up to heaven, but was beating his breast and saying, "God, be merciful to me, a sinner!" I tell you, this man went down to his home justified rather than the other; for all who exalt themselves will be humbled, but all who humble themselves will be exalted.' (Luke 18.10–14)

This sermon had quite an impact, but I sensed that most of those who heard it ultimately missed the point. There were many people in the church passionate about serving marginalized people, as evidenced by the church's commitment to the food bank and winter night shelter for homeless people – both very important ministries that are highly commendable. And yet broken people were still seen as people 'out there' that the church needed to welcome in. We had not yet grasped that we were all broken people.

Let us imagine two people going to church, one successful in their career, married with many children; the other broken and grieving. The first might pray: 'God, I thank you for the many blessings you have given me: my partner, my children, the income that supports us. Please help this grieving person and all those who suffer.' The one who is broken by grief might not even look up to heaven in prayer; they might struggle to sing songs of worship; perhaps they might pray: 'God, be merciful to me, I am in despair!' What if this second person – this broken, grieving person, who struggles to utter any words in prayer, who struggles to contemplate hope – what if they were not the one who needed to change?

Notes

1 RSA, 2013, 'RSA Replay – The Power of Vulnerability', *YouTube*, first broadcast 4 July 2013, www.youtube.com/watch?v=QMzBv35H bLk, accessed 17.1.2020.

Acknowledgements

The tutors of Regent's Park College, Oxford, gave me the tools to reflect on my experience before God – a gift beyond measure. Thanks in particular to the MTh tutors who first introduced me to pastoral theology. The Revd Dr Paul Beasley-Murray was my first pastor and was instrumental in my ministerial formation. Thank you for giving me the firm biblical, theological and pastoral foundations that have kept me rooted through many storms. Many medical staff were involved in my diagnosis and treatment, and in helping me manage the anxiety that accompanied it. You were not only efficient, but you were kind, and that made all the difference. The Revd Alison Taylor kept me going through an intolerable situation by her friendship and down-to-earth advice. Alison, you were a Godsend. My church's leadership team showed me love and grace when I was at my lowest, allowing me the time I needed to grieve. I will not forget their kindness. The British Library became my place of pilgrimage during this time of grieving – thanks to the staff for providing me with such a beautiful place to read, write and, occasionally, to cry (though not on the books). Thanks to Sarah Laurie for reading an early draft of this book, for encouraging me to finish the manuscript, and for pointing me to the work of Jody Day. Kevin Ellis's work inspired my own and I am most grateful for his advice and encouragement. Thanks to Jacky Maggs for proofreading the final manuscript through tears. Thank you to SCM Press for taking a risk on a first-time author. Finally, thank you to Derek, who has always cared more about my suffering than his own.

Bibliography

Barton, John and Julia Bowden, 2004, *The Original Story: God, Israel and the World*, London: Darton, Longman and Todd.

Brown, Brené, 2007, *I Thought It Was Just Me: Women Reclaiming Power and Courage in a Culture of Shame*, New York: Penguin.

Brown, Colin, 1978, 'Resurrection' in Colin Brown (ed.), *The New International Dictionary of New Testament Theology Vol. 3*, Exeter: Paternoster Press, pp. 259–309.

Brueggemann, Walter, 1982, *Genesis*, Interpretation: A Bible Commentary for Teaching and Preaching, Louisville, KY: Westminster John Knox Press.

Cain, Madelyn, 2001, *The Childless Revolution: What It Means to Be Childless Today*, New York: Perseus.

Choices in childlessness: the report of a working party set up in July 1979 under the auspices of the Free Church Federal Council and the British Council of Churches, London: Free Church Federal Council, 1982.

Craddock, Fred B., 1990, *Luke*, Interpretation: A Bible Commentary for Teaching and Preaching, Louisville, KY: Westminster John Knox Press.

Crenshaw, James L., 2010, *Old Testament Wisdom: An Introduction*, 3rd edn, Louisville, KY: Westminster John Knox Press.

Day, Jody, 2016, *Living the Life Unexpected: How to Find Hope, Meaning and a Fulfilling Future* Without *Children*, London: Pan Macmillan, Kindle edition.

Eiesland, Nancy, 1994, *The Disabled God*, Nashville, TN: Abingdon Press.

Ellis, Christopher J. and Myra Blyth (eds) for The Baptist Union of Great Britain, 2005, *Gathering for Worship: Patterns and Prayers for the Community of Disciples*, Norwich: Canterbury Press.

Ellis, Kevin, 2003, 'Searching for an impotent God', *Contact* 141(1), pp. 11–16.

Ellis, Kevin, 2006, *Christianity and Childlessness*, Cambridge: Grove Books.

Ellis, Kevin, 2013, 'Invisible Pain' in Jennifer Tann (ed.), *Soul Pain: Priests Reflect on Personal Experiences of Serious and Terminal Illness*, Norwich: Canterbury Press, pp. 129–45.

Fox, Michael V., 1999, *A Time to Tear Down and a Time to Build Up: A Rereading of Ecclesiastes*, Grand Rapids, MI: William B. Eerdmans.

Hilborn, D., 1994, 'For the Procreation of Children' in S. Durber (ed.), *As Man and Woman Made*, London: United Reformed Church.

Jones, Serene, 2009, *Trauma and Grace: Theology in a Ruptured World*, Louisville, KY: Westminster John Knox Press.

Kaiser, Otto, 1995, 'Qoheleth' in J. Day, R. P. Gordon and H. G. M. Williamson (eds), *Wisdom in Ancient Israel: Essays in Honour of J.A. Emerton*, Cambridge: Cambridge University Press.

Kübler-Ross, Elisabeth, 1969, *On Death and Dying: What the Dying Have to Teach Doctors, Nurses, Clergy and Their Own Families*, 50th anniversary edition, New York: Scribner, Kindle edition.

Kübler-Ross, Elisabeth and David Kessler, 2005, *On Grief and Grieving: Finding the Meaning of Grief Through the Five Stages of Loss*, London: Simon & Schuster, Kindle edition.

Kushner, Harold S., 1981, *When Bad Things Happen to Good People*, 20th anniversary edition, London: Pan Books, Kindle edition.

Lewis, Alan, 2001, *Between Cross and Resurrection*, Grand Rapids, MI: William B. Eerdmans.

Lewis, C. S., 1942, *The Screwtape Letters*, London: Geoffrey Bles.

Lewis, C. S., 1955, *The Magician's Nephew*, London: Fontana Lions, 15th impression.

Lisle, L., 1999, *Without Child: Challenging the Stigma of Childlessness*, London: Routledge.

Lowrie, Lizzie, 2020, *Salt Water and Honey: Lost Dreams, Good Grief and a Better Story*, Milton Keynes: Authentic.

McGuinness, G. B., 1995, 'Childlessness' in David J. Atkinson and David H. Field (eds), *New Dictionary of Christian Ethics and Pastoral Theology*, Leicester: Inter-Varsity Press.

McKeown, John, 2014, *God's Babies: Natalism and Bible Interpretation in Modern America*, Cambridge: Open Book Publishers.

Morgan, Rosemary, 2013, *Living with Infertility – A Christian Perspective*, Abingdon: The Bible Reading Fellowship.

Moss, Candida R. and Joel S. Baden, 2015, *Reconceiving Infertility: Biblical Perspectives on Procreation and Childlessness*, Princeton, NJ: Princeton University Press.

O'Donnell, Karen, 2019, 'Theology and reproductive loss', *Modern Believing* 60, 2, pp. 123–32.

Perry, Philippa, 2019, *The Book You Wish Your Parents Had Read (and Your Children Will be Glad That You Did)*, London: Penguin Life.

Roach, Jason and Philippa Taylor, 2014, *Facing Infertility: Guidance for Christian Couples Considering IVF*, London: Christian Medical Fellowship.

Rollins, Pete, 2009, *The Orthodox Heretic: And Other Impossible Tales*, Norwich: Canterbury Press.

Ruhi-López, Angelique and Carmen Santamaría, 2012, *The Infertility Companion for Catholics: Spiritual and Practical Support for Couples*, Notre Dame, IN: Ave Maria Press.

Sittser, Jerry, 2004, *A Grace Disguised: How the Soul Grows through Loss*, Grand Rapids, MI: Zondervan.

Spring, Beth, 1989, *Childless: The Hurt and the Hope*, Oxford: Lion Publishing.

Tolkien, J. R. R., 1954, *The Fellowship of the Ring*, London: George Allen & Unwin.

Trible, Phyllis, 1976, 'Two Women in a Man's World: A Reading of the Book of Ruth', *Soundings: An Interdisciplinary Journal* 59(3), pp. 251–79.

Trible, Phyllis, 1978, *God and the Rhetoric of Sexuality*, Philadelphia, PA: Fortress Press.

Trible, Phyllis, 1992, *Texts of Terror: Literary-Feminist Readings of Biblical Narratives*, London: SCM Press.

Twenge, Jean M., 2012, *The Impatient Woman's Guide to Getting Pregnant*, New York: Simon & Schuster.

Tyler May, E., 1995, *Barren in the Promised Land: Childless Americans and the Pursuit of Happiness*, Cambridge, MA: Harvard University Press.

Vanier, Jean, 1998, *Becoming Human*, Toronto: House of Anansi Press.

Voysey, Sheridan, 2013, *Resurrection Year: Turning Broken Dreams into New Beginnings*, Nashville, TN: Thomas Nelson.

Walton, Heather, 1999, 'Passion and pain: conceiving theology out of infertility', *Contact* 130(1), pp. 3–9.

Walton, Heather, 2003, 'Advent: theological reflections on IVF', *Theology and Sexuality* 9(2), pp. 201–9.

Warner, Meg, 2019, '"Sing, O barren one who did not bear": childlessness, blessing and vocation in the Old Testament', *Modern Believing* 60(2), pp. 111–21.

Warnock, Mary, 2002, *Making Babies: Is There a Right to Have Children?*, Oxford: Oxford University Press.

Whybray, R. N., 1989, *The New Century Bible Commentary: Ecclesiastes*, London: Marshall, Morgan & Scott.

Wilkinson, David, 2002, *The Message of Creation: Encountering the Lord of the Universe*, The Bible Speaks Today, Leicester: Inter-Varsity Press.

Winston, Robert, 2015, *The Essential Fertility Guide*, London: Quadrille.

Working Group of Human Embryology and Early Human Life for the Methodist Church, 2008, *Created in God's Image: An Ecumenical Report on Contemporary Challenges and Principles relating to Early Human Life*, downloaded from www.methodist.org.uk.

Websites

www.bbc.co.uk
www.chasingcreation.org
www.churchtimes.co.uk
www.cmf.org.uk
www.edwinasandys.com
www.emilymcdowell.com
www.fourkindsofchristmas.com
www.fertilitynetworkuk.org
www.hfea.gov.uk
www.methodist.org.uk
www.miscarriageassociation.org.uk
www.mumsnet.com
www.mypoint.tv
www.nhs.uk
www.robinhadley.co.uk/
www.saltwaterandhoney.org
www.songselect.ccli.com
www.theguardian.com
www.twitter.com
www.vatican.va
www.youtube.com
www.worldchildlessweek.net

Podcasts

Drawing the Line: When IVF Doesn't Work, first broadcast on 29 May
   2015 on BBC Radio 4, www.bbc.co.uk/programmes/b05w85g1
Infertile AF by Alison Prato, https://infertileaf.libsyn.com
Sounds True, www.resources.soundstrue.com/
What happens when IVF doesn't work? Live Wires, Radio 5 Live,
   released 1 November 2019, www.bbc.co.uk/sounds/play/p07sr58c

Index